THE BEST

WRITING

—ON—

WRITING

THE BEST

WRITING

—ON—

WRITING

EDITED BY JACK HEFFRON

STORY PRESS

CINCINNATI, OHIO

98 97 96 95 94   5 4 3 2 1

Library of Congress Cataloging-in-Publication Data

The best writing on writing / edited by Jack Heffron.
     p.   cm.
  Includes index.
  ISBN 1-884910-01-7
  1. Authorship. I. Heffron, Jack.
PN151.B58   1994
808'.02 — dc20   94-13864
                                                   CIP

Designed by Clare Finney

PERMISSIONS

CONTENTS

INTRODUCTION

Imagine a meeting of today's top writers. They're trading tips and opinions about their craft, talking about new ideas and controversial trends, discussing pieces they've just finished or intend to start. They're recounting struggles with their work, debating current issues, laughing at each other's stories. And you're right with them, hearing every word.

The Best Writing on Writing offers you that opportunity. In this book, you will find 1993's finest, liveliest, most provocative and enlightening essays, articles, lectures and book excerpts on the subject of writing. The selections will inform and inspire you, delight and entertain you.

The twenty-seven writers featured here cover a broad range of topics: fiction, nonfiction, poetry, playwriting and screenwriting. Some update you on current trends. In "It's a Bad Time Out There for Emotion," Edna O'Brien argues that writers today too often rely on irony rather than on feeling. James Fenton questions the motives, and the insight, of poets who write more for their resumes than their readers in "Mistakes People Make About Poetry." Natalia Rachel Singer, in "Nonfiction in First Person, Without Apology," celebrates the emergence of creative nonfiction, in which writers can use the "I" with pride.

Others offer practical instruction. Diane Lefer, for example, teaches you how to plot stories in new ways in "Breaking the 'Rules' of Story Structure." Ann Beattie explains the sources of her story people in "Where Characters Come From." Edward Albee and Tony Kushner reveal their methods of writing plays.

Some of the selections confront issues that confront writers. In "The Way We Write Now," Sharon Oard Warner feels that writers too often hide behind inference and indirection when writing about AIDS. Ayanna Black cites the struggles and toasts the successes of minority writers in "Inglish: Writing With an Accent." Adrienne Rich examines the political poem—its limitations and its possibilities—in "Someone Is Writing a Poem."

Bonnie Friedman ponders the moral and ethical complexities of writing about those we know and love in "Your Mother's Passions, Your Sister's Woes: Writing About the Living."

Others look at the writer's life. James Michener shares his trove of writerly wisdom in "Lessons of a Lifetime," while Kim R. Stafford, in the touching "My Father's Place," gives us the lessons he learned from his father, poet William Stafford.

This variety of subjects is matched by a variety of voices. In her very funny "Passing the Torch," Candyce Barnes remembers her first brush with literary fame and fortune—at age eight. Donald Hall, on the other hand, offers a deeply moving account of how his fight with colon cancer has changed his life as a writer in "The Books Not Read, the Lines Not Written: A Poet Confronts His Mortality." David Freeman humorously takes on the language of Hollywood in "The Screenwriter's Lexicon," while William Kittredge issues a no-nonsense call for authentic writing about the West in "Death of the Western."

To collect these pieces, I searched hundreds of periodicals—newspapers, consumer magazines, literary magazines, trade journals, house organs for writers' organizations. I spoke to heads of writers' conferences. I read every book on the subject I could find. But I could not have assembled this collection without the help of many people. Magazine editors generously shipped their 1993 issues, while book editors took time to send requested copies. Kind-hearted librarians lugged a year's worth of issues from the archives. And many teachers, editors and writers offered guidance on where to look, who to call, what to read. To all of these people who lent their time and advice, I'm truly grateful.

The result of these efforts: *The Best Writing on Writing*. It's the first volume in a regular series from Story Press—a meeting of writers, discussing what they do best, for all of us who love the written word.

—Jack Heffron

CANDYCE BARNES

PASSING THE TORCH

TWO WRITING LIVES

Seems like almost everybody at one time or another has taken a notion to be a writer. It seemed to me when I was younger that it must be a very mysterious undertaking. Pictures I'd seen of writers showed bristly men who had the same pained look my Texas uncle had mornings before he took a tot of his "phlegm cutter." Lady writers looked sickly or demented. Still, I'd longed to meet the genuine article until, in the third grade, I entered the field myself.

It was poetry that set me on the road to ruin. A poetry contest sponsored by the Memphis *Commercial Appeal*. By age eight, I'd written a poem to our dog, to the Memphis State basketball team, and to my grandmother's canary. My credentials as the writer in the family were firmly established. Fortunately that contest came along just about when I reached my poetic peak. Fate drew me ever closer to the writing life — since this is a love story, that's OK. Since it's going to be a true story, I'm bound to tell you it was years before I got paid for writing anything again. The prize was fame, which in the third grade meant your picture in the paper, and a modest fortune. Five dollars as I recall.

I was pretty nonchalant about my creative powers in those days. I didn't wait for any old muse to beget inspiration, I just looked out the window and started to write. Some years ago in Bardstown, Kentucky, my husband and I visited the house in which Stephen Foster wrote "My Old Kentucky Home"; in the foyer there was a mural of Stephen being visited by his muse: a hefty broad of Wagnerian proportions. She looked pissed off, like she was fixing to shake him and slap him good if he didn't come up with something right this minute. I was profoundly grateful that I'd given up writing poetry (I hear the muse strikes poets most often), and it certainly convinced me to write only about what I saw and heard and knew.

What I saw, lo those many years ago, was a robin building a nest. I'd been raised a Southern Baptist, and the hymnals are nothing if not chock full of rhyme and galloping meter. So once I had "Here is a bird building her nest . . . ," it was only a matter of time until, "Building the kind that she likes best . . . ," followed as night the day. There was a nice bit about "putting sticks here and putting sticks there," and a thrilling denouement when the nest was "ready for the baby birds," and the mother was "too excited for words." With almost indecent haste, within a stanza I think, the baby birds had up and flown. My grasp of bird biology might have been suspect, but I like to think that even then, I had a handle on dramatic pacing. To hell with the muse: write out of your own window and keep 'em moving.

I won. I also learned that every triumph carries the seed of its own disaster. Come time for the big picture in the paper and my mother made me wear the dress I hated most in the world. I *still* hate that dress. It was white with black polka dots. The bodice was a black peasant-style jerkin that laced shut. It had puffed sleeves and a sash. I had been planning something along the lines of a cowboy hat and holsters. Later I got even with that dress by swelling up and busting it loose on the playground.

I acquired important knowledge: the written word could get you out of school. Part of the festivities required that I read my poem to an Audience. I was a luncheon guest of the Ladies' Poetry Society at the Nineteenth Century Club. Certainly rarified literary air for a junior outlaw. I shared the podium with Dr. Margaret Moore Jacobs. In those days, O Best Beloved, all lady poets had three names. Her house even had three names: Dear Little House. I am not making this up. The audience swelled with ample bosom and ample hat, Margaret Moore Jacobs hugged me to the vast and pillowy tundra that was her chest, gave me a signed copy of *Happiness Always* ("To a Poetess"), and I felt the torch had been passed. The whole day smelled of lavender. Years later I saw Helen Hokinson's cartoons and found out where I'd been.

I spent my five dollars on a slingshot, a tomahawk, and some plastic horses. But I had found true love. From that day forth, I would be a Writer. I would, by God, get three names if I had to. I've kept reading and learning the tricky bits of this craft even though I ditched poetry in college shortly after my T.S. Eliot period. As it turned out, "Birdnest" really had been my peak. Still, I've always been grateful for that first heady confirmation of myself as a Writer. A Poetess.

It wasn't but a month or so ago that a group I'm a member of sponsored a writing and art contest for kids in the first through sixth grades. OK, we're called Greenheads, it's an environmental group, and nobody has big boobs (I do have quite a collection of hats, including cowboy). The little girl who won the writing award (twenty-five dollars and a Greenheads T-shirt) was in the first grade, and at the ceremony she seemed a bit subdued. Finally her mother sidled over and told me: "She's mad because I made her wear a dress." The torch has been passed.

DONALD HALL

THE BOOKS NOT READ, THE LINES NOT WRITTEN: A POET CONFRONTS HIS MORTALITY

THE NEW YORK TIMES BOOK REVIEW

My life's project began in the second grade when I was seven and whooping cough kept me home from school. I grew bored with radio soap operas of the 1930's. They were 15 minutes long, telling stories about Ma Perkins or Mary Noble, Backstage Wife. I had brought my storybook home from school in Connecticut; in my boredom I read it over and over. Thus I became fluent at reading for the first time, and discovered the bliss of abandonment to print, to word and story. From the love of reading eventually derived the desire to write, a lifelong commitment to making things that might (if I were diligent, talented and lucky) resemble the books I love reading.

Reading and writing have filled the days of my life, good times and bad ones, reflecting passages of love, despair, anger and joy. Reading and writing take their places even in mourning and in fear of death. Through words I remember my first consciousness of mortality. When I was nine and a great-aunt died, I lay in bed after the funeral, staying awake to repeat a sentence in my head: "Now death has become a reality." It was as if I were reading my biography, and "at the age of nine," the book said, "death became a reality for Donald Hall."

A couple of years later, I read over and over again a novel called *Jimmy Sharswood*, by Roy Helton, a North Carolina poet (I found out later) whom Robert Frost admired. The eponymous boy-hero dies, and I reread the book in order to weep, not to escape from mortality but to embrace it — or at least embrace the idea of it. Maybe one pursues literary death in order to evade the real thing. Samuel Taylor Coleridge noted a fear that afflicts the scrupulous literary mind: "Poetry—excites us to artificial feelings—callous to real ones."

Whatever the reason, when I find someone's death insupportable, I look to poetry. I find solace in entering someone else's grief, intense as the moment's shudder, across centuries or even across languages and cultures. A poem I first look for is "The Exequy" by Henry King. King, who was John Donne's executor, lived from 1592 to 1669; in 1617 he married Ann Berkeley when she was 17; she died at 24 and King addressed her in tetrameter couplets:

> Never shall I
> Be so much blest as to descry
> A glimpse of thee, till that day come
> Which shall the earth to cinders doome,
> And a fierce feaver must calcine
> The body of this world like thine,
> (My little world!)

His grief over the young woman dead of a fever is more painful than this morning's obituary page; and always my misery takes dour satisfaction in Henry King's company.

Much poetry makes itself out of wretchedness, an energetic conflict: the pleasure of language assaults even as it embodies a statement of misery. This applies to even the oldest poetry: reading a translation from the Sumerian, we hear the lament of Gilgamesh, wretched over the death of his blood brother Enkidu. These words come from the Penguin prose translation by N.K. Sandars: Gilgamesh "began to rage like a lion, like a lioness robbed of her whelps. This way and that he paced round the bed, he tore out his hair and strewed it around. . . . Seven days and seven nights he wept for Enkidu, until the worm fastened on him. Only then he gave him up to the earth."

Three thousand years later, we have all endured the same wild or petulant grief.

And what do we next endure or feel? When we grieve for

another we always grieve for ourselves. Gilgamesh says: "What my brother is now, that shall I be when I am dead." Even for Henry King, although his Christianity is confident of survival, his bride's death leads to thoughts of his own:

Thou wilt not wake
Till I thy fate shall overtake:
Till age, or grief, or sickness must
Marry my body to that dust
It so much loves; and fill the room
My heart keeps empty in thy tomb.
Stay for me there: I will not fail
To meet thee in that hallow vale.

It is a matter of course, in the lives we endure, that each of us must one day acknowledge forthcoming death — unless we drop of an unpredicted heart attack or a random bullet. One day we will hear the oncologist say, "I'm afraid the prognosis is discouraging."

Almost four years ago a young doctor with thick glasses cleared his throat before he told me, "You have colon cancer." After the operation my chances of making five years were two out of three, but last year the carcinoma metastasized to my liver. With two-thirds of that organ removed, together with all discernible disease, my chances have dwindled to one in three. From day to day I feel healthy and energetic; I am happy in work and love; it is a good patch of my life. But every quarter I have blood work done, and I am aware that one day the results will likely bear bad tidings.

It is not grief that one feels for oneself but dread of the grief of others. (I do not speak out of altruism.) Doubtless I fear the pain of dying, but when I expect my own death, mostly I feel not fear or dread but black sadness that my daily routine must conclude; no more glancing through *The Boston Globe* early in the morning while drinking black coffee; no more bodily love; no more working at the desk all day — the long engagement with language, which I adore as a sculptor loves wood or clay, as a musician melody and tempo; no more sleepy visions of the Red Sox losing another game as I go to bed.

And no more reading. Approaching death touches on reading as on everything else. For one thing, reading will not distract us from dread. Oh, if we merely foresee the moment of ether and the knife, certain books may occupy us. Before my first large operation, gallbladder in 1969, I read "Portnoy's Complaint." I laughed, page by page, until the orderlies rolled me to the operating room. But then I couldn't finish the book for a month; when an incision is healing, we avoid books that make us laugh.

With my recent diseases and operations, surgery has been my least concern. When they make the incision, what will they *find*? What will the laboratory's dyes and microscopes discover, peering at cell structure? Not even Philip Roth distracts from such concerns; not even spy sagas or horror books. For that matter, I cannot read junk for diversion. Finer sensibilities than my own have relaxed with Agatha Christie or Zane Grey—but under conditions of pain and distress, slack language causes me pain and distress.

What can we read, then, in mortal circumstances? I cannot concentrate enough to read Linda Gregg's poems or Flaubert's letters to George Sand or Nicholas Grimal's new history of old Egypt; the words of others quickly metamorphose into my own anxieties, and I read two pages without reading a sentence. John Gospel I can take a few verses at a time; his doctrines of love raise me up—but then his concentration on last things cuts to the bone.

Depressed over my probable brevity, I find my reading mocked by my own acquisitiveness. Part of my pleasure in reading has always been pride in accumulation. I read to use what I read, for understanding and for writing; take away that future use, and my reading mocks me: if I am not to live more than a wretched year or two, what I am reading *for*? I should be able to read for the joy of a book's beauty but I cannot. For the first time in my life, reading depresses me; the old comforts fall away; I might as well feel miserable watching Vanna White spin a wheel.

For weeks after my last operation—frail and without energy, sleeping 10 hours—I looked in my house at all the books I had not read and wept for my inability to read them. Or I looked at great books I had read too quickly in my avidity—telling myself that I would return to them later. There is never a *later*, but for most of my life I have believed in *later*.

Wherever I turned to escape depression, the place I turned to became the place I had left. When I found comfort in love, love turned bitter with the notion of abandoning it. King Gilgamesh, realizing that what had happened to Enkidu would happen to him, journeyed to the end of the earth—with much suffering, overcoming terrible obstacles—to seek counsel of the one man who had avoided dying, a Babylonian Noah called Utnapishtim. But Utnapishtim could not pass immortality on.

Like reading, writing has always provided a dream of acquisition: so many poems, so many books. After my last operation I had a book of my own to finish, "Life Work," half-drafted when I learned about my liver. There were children's books begun, with grandchildren on my mind. There were poems to work over, if I had time. A new poem, out of my illness, began nibbling at the edges of consciousness.

Three and a half weeks after my operation, I returned to "Life Work"; then I started on the new poem; then I took up old poems again—changing a word, altering a line break or a mark of punctuation. At first I worked only in brief intent bursts, 10 or 20 minutes, trying to tidy things up. Working again I forgot the statistics of survival—for minutes on end, then for hours. Able to write, I was able to read again—to return to Adam Smith's "Wealth of Nations," which I had interrupted; to read Charles Simic's new poems; to reread Anton Chekhov's stories about the lives and deaths, miserable and exalted, of every man and every woman.

DIANE LEFER

BREAKING THE "RULES" OF STORY STRUCTURE

NOVEL AND SHORT STORY WRITER'S MARKET

Several years ago, I worked with a creative writing student who produced stylish, astute literary criticism but kept turning in conventionally plotted stories that clunked their way to pat conclusions. Finally I confronted him. "What happens to all your sophistication when you sit down to write fiction?" He explained he'd once been told to pack it away until he'd mastered the so-called basics: "You have to learn to write a traditional story before you begin to experiment." To me that's like saying a musical person with great fingers but no breath control has to master the trumpet before trying the piano.

There's a mistaken premise here. The "basics" to me include attention to language, convincing characterizations, a sense of discovery and surprise, insights that make the reader stop and marvel, prose that lives and tells the truth.

QUESTIONING THE TRADITIONAL STORY

There's nothing second-rate about a traditional story. Lots of people write great ones and millions of people love to read them. For some writers, though, the form itself may feel unnatural, not suited to portraying the complexities of a world marked by ambiguity and dislocations, chaos and incongruities, where answers are suspect and bizarre juxtapositions a part of daily life. Before beginning a story, you might ask yourself:

- Do I want to go beyond telling what happened and re-create the feeling?

- Am I as interested in inner life as in outward action?

- Am I as curious to find out what a character is going to say or think next as in the next turn of the plot?

- Do I take pleasure in what Franz Kafka called "the mind reveling in its own keenness?"

- Do I pay attention to language itself and judge stories — including my own — not just on how they read on the page, but out loud?

- Do I often discover what I'm writing about only in the process of writing?

- Do I tend to order events by their emotional or psychological links rather than their chronology?

- Do I think we can best approach Truth through intuition, through hints and suggestions, that Truth flees at any direct approach?

If you answered yes to many of these questions, you probably find traditional structure confining, an obstacle to expression instead of a helpful guide. You're not alone. Consider some of the writers and readers who have questioned the premises many of us take for granted.

The traditional story revolves around a conflict. This is a requirement Ursula LeGuin disparages as the "gladiatorial view of fiction."

The movement of the story progresses from rising action to climax to the falling off of the denouement. Hmmm, say the feminist literary critics. Sounds suspiciously like male sexual response. Which is *not*, they note, the only way to satisfy a reader. (This doesn't mean for a moment that only women will reject the standard progression: Kafka began "The Metamorphosis" with the most dramatic moment: "As Gregor Samsa awoke one morning from uneasy dreams he found himself transformed in his bed into a gigantic insect." I can just imagine a modern-day workshop leader telling Kafka that this transformation is clearly the climactic moment and must happen near the *end*. But Kafka—like many contemporary writers who wonder how ordinary life goes on after great trauma—is not concerned with the hows and whys of the unthinkable cataclysmic event, but rather its aftermath.

In modern fiction, it's strange to talk about story climax anyway. These days, stories often end with a subtle realization or epiphany rather than rockets going off. As a result, the edgy juxtapositions and pulsing rhythms of an unconventional story may actually be more engaging to readers than the traditionally structured build-up to a quiet or inconclusive resolution.

A main character must undergo a change. (I like to imagine Kafka walking out of a workshop before starting to write "The Metamorphosis." "You want change?" he mutters. "All right, I'll give you change!") My objection is that life experience teaches us an equally dramatic (if frustrating) truth: In spite of conflict, confrontation and crisis, people often don't, can't or won't change.

SOME ALTERNATIVE METAPHORS

Critics have compared Amy Hempel's stories to *mosaics*: She provides scenes and information in bits and pieces until the whole picture comes together. I would go further and say she strategically leaves a few key scenes out, so that the reader must participate in the creation. In her powerful story "In the Cemetery Where Al Jolson Is Buried" (from *Reasons to Live*, Alfred A. Knopf, 1985), the narrator recalls her visits to a dying friend and her inability to give all the desired support. We never see a confrontation between the two young women; though we know it happens, there's no account of the death; there's no funeral. Can't you just hear the workshop complaint: Amy, you're avoiding the emotion. Precisely! The reader must fill in the incidents too painful for the narrator to recount. The story ends with a series of memories and anecdotes that bring home an emotional understanding of the narrator's sense of threat, uncertainty, guilt and grief.

I've heard author William Least Heat-Moon use the metaphor of a *wheel* to describe Native American storytelling. The heart of the story is the hub of the wheel. The storyteller moves around the circumference a bit, then down one of the spokes to touch the hub, then back to the circumference, approaching the heart again and again from different points. As with Hempel's mosaic, the listener or reader shares in the effort of creation until all points on the circumference are connected, every spoke leads to the hub, the whole wheel is filled in.

A story that seems to work this way is "The Water-Faucet Vision" by Gish Jen, first published in *Nimrod*, reprinted in *Best American Short Stories 1988* (Houghton Mifflin) and later forming part of Jen's novel *Typical American* (Houghton Mifflin, 1991). The hub is a desire, the idea of seeking comfort for the pains of life. The circumference represents the narrator Callie's life history as she grows up in a turbulent Chinese-American family, attends Catholic school and longs to be a martyred miracle-working saint, reaches adulthood and mourns her mother's death. The narrative jumps around in time, i.e., all over the circumference of the wheel, but whatever its starting point, every anecdote and every memory becomes another spoke leading to the desire for comfort. Every moment recounted connects to the hub, the heart that is the yearning for belief, for a time when — in the story's closing words — "one had only to direct the hand of the Almighty and say, just here, Lord, we hurt here — and here, and here and here."

MORE METAPHORS

A jazz musician may seem to go all over the place in a *musical improvisation*, but there's always an underlying structure to return to. The sense of liberating spontaneity is exhilarating when matched by technical proficiency and control. That's the feeling I got from Sandra Cisneros' collection, *Women Hollering Creek and Other Stories* (Random House, 1991), a series of Mexican-American vernacular solos of such spilling-forth immediacy they feel effortless though the careful crafting and choice of language and image make it clear they were not. In many of these short short stories—some no more than a page or two in length—Cisneros states an idea or image in the first sentence, flies away with it and returns to the same image (the way a musician returns to a chord) to ground the story in the end. One story opens and closes with language reminiscent of a nostalgic ballad; another reads like a *ranchera*-style love song written in paragraphs instead of stanzas. Some stories in the collection (the most self-conscious and least successful, I think) are longer, more traditional and more sustained; some are like overheard gossip sessions. The overall effect made me think of attending a concert in a plaza, walking into the church or movie theater, watching people and listening to their chatter in between songs. Cisneros even ends the book with a brass instrument flourish: "¡tan Tan!"

Tim O'Brien's "How to Tell a True War Story" (from *The Things They Carried*, Houghton Mifflin/Seymour Lawrence, 1990) makes devastating use of *instant replay*. O'Brien holds up the memory of a terrible moment in Vietnam: A man is blown up by a landmine. At such times, O'Brien writes, "The angles of vision are skewed. . . . The pictures get jumbled; you tend to miss a lot," and so he tells it again and again, differently each time, obsessed by the incident and by trying to tell it truly. The story's unconventional structure (replay—authorial commentary—replay—commentary) forces the fascinated and horrified reader to face the relentless intensity and impossible-to-resolve contradictions of war.

Marlene Nourbese Philip's "Burn Sugar" (anthologized in *International Feminist Fiction*, Crossing Press, 1992) is a *process* story, focused not on what happens, but how. The action is simple: The narrator, a Caribbean-born woman now living in Canada, bakes a cake from a family recipe while remembering her mother's kitchen. She describes the beating hand, the batter stiffening in resistance, the disappearance and blending of ingredients. At the same time, the language of the narrative switches between Caribbean and Canadian English. The very process of baking the cake is metaphoric on different levels, all having to do with cultural transformation and survival as well as the conflicted relationship between mother and daughter. The process bridges cultures, past and present, mother and daughter. This doesn't happen *in* the story, but rather *through* it.

If a story that rises to a climax and then falls off is "male," what sort of story would illustrate *female textual/sexual response*? Could it be a story that peaks again and again, in which waves of excitement and satisfaction are diffused throughout the text instead of being focused on a single moment near the end? Is it a story in which individual themes and incidents connect up in a sense of union or unity instead of resulting in a clear-cut choice or a change?

What "happens" in Kate Braverman's chillingly seductive story "Winter Blues" (*Squandering the Blue*, Fawcett Columbine, 1990) is deceptively simple. The protagonist, Erica, works on a college paper about contemporary American poets while her bored daughter demands attention. As far as plot goes, that's it. But what really happens is that Braverman weaves together several themes and makes them cohere into a frightening vision. The Chernobyl nuclear accident hangs like a threat over the story; the poets Erica writes about are suicidal and self-destructive; shocking memories of life with her drug-addicted husband surface as Erica tries to keep her young child distracted. The elements of the story are not related through logic or cause and effect but through image and incantatory almost hallucinogenic prose. Poets wear "their diseases like garlands," the blood of Los Angeles is "a red neon wash, a kind of sea of autistic traffic lights," the Hawaiian sky is the "pink of irradiated flamingos," and children are taught not to touch flame: "Then we touch it."

WHY LOOK FOR METAPHOR?

Obviously the alternative metaphors I've cited overlap and are not the only possibilities. But be forewarned. In reliance on metaphor, sound and rhythm, careful and evocative word choice, intuitive links, unexpected juxtapositions and suggestion instead of statement, the unconventional story uses many of the techniques of poetry, an art form many people in our society, alas, disdain. If you choose this route, you'll have to expect a specific kind of rejection on occasion: the stodgy editor who sniffs, "This isn't a story, it's a prose poem," as if poetic effect doesn't enrich a story but rather diminishes it!

Why do I look for metaphors and invent labels? Isn't that just as arbitrary and rule-bound as following conventional form?

Our brains are wired so that thinking often takes the path of least resistance, the most worn path. (I suspect that's one reason why we may end up with pat, predictable stories when we follow the most traditional structure. We may shunt our most original insights and deepest intuition off onto unused branch lines as we barrel down the familiar track.) Once alternative structures have been brought into conscious awareness — something metaphor can do in a suggestive rather than a dogmatic way — they become internalized, part of our psychic inventory. We can intuitively select the best form for our material without always falling back on the same old scheme.

IT HAPPENS BECAUSE IT HAS TO

I don't sit down and think I'm going to write a male story today, or a female story. (Anyway, I think most great stories are androgynous, with both "male" and "female" attributes. It's not a question of exclusion, but rather of emphasis.) An alternative structure usually appears naturally as a story develops — because it *has* to. I may not even recognize the controlling metaphor until I start revising. Then I'll use the model to help shape the story and make the elements cohere, to lessen the danger that an intuitively written story will end up too scattered or random and meaningless to anyone but the author. For example, in a mosaic story, each constituent piece has its own boundaries, its own shape. I'll try to see that each separate incident has a small but noticeable climactic moment. I'll alternate dramatic incidents with digressions, meditations or sections that explore the inner workings of a character's mind. All these separate pieces are held together because they are inside the same frame and — to mix a metaphor — because the same search or question or metaphor or symbol runs through all, like a thread through the hearts of many beads.

CONTINUITY VS. CHANGE

Consider one of history's great transformations, when Saul, the persecutor of Christians, became Paul, who practically created Christianity as an institution and church. But it's not unreasonable to interpret Paul's story this way: that he was vigorous, zealous and single-minded both before and after the transformative experience. So much for change!

Still, if fictional characters appear the same at beginning and end, they're likely to seem sculpted rather than alive, and that can make a story static. But if there has to be a turning point, why not make it a shift in the *reader*? What if the *reader* changes and comes to see a character or a situation in a new light?

One day, I shocked myself by joining in a conversation complaining about the younger generation. When I was an adolescent, I swore I'd never forget what it was like to be a kid and would never judge teenagers cruelly or put them down, but there I was, doing just that. I reacted to my treachery by writing "What She Stood For" (*The Literary Review*, Fall, 1991, collected in *The Circles I Move In*, Zoland Books). I started out by intentionally repeating and illustrating all the common negative stereotypes I had attributed to today's teens, saddling my protagonist, Kendra, with her shallow shopping mall mentality, her lack of values, her flirtation with violence, her emotionally disconnected sexuality. But as I wrote, I tried to see her point of view, and found myself bringing her environment to life with all its contradictions and hypocrisy, its background of terrible but half-understood world events and troubled adults. In the course of the story, Kendra began to look almost heroic to me, striving and yearning for something better, sometimes choosing self-defeating paths because she hadn't yet been able to see any others. Kendra didn't so much change, as show her shifting shape — formed by the interplay of her own intrinsic qualities and outside forces — and her possibilities. I'd begun by dismissing, despising and satirizing her. I hope that readers changed their views as I did: first separating themselves from Kendra, laughing bitterly and shaking their heads with despair but eventually identifying with her struggle for self, fervently hoping she would not just survive but thrive.

CREATING OUT OF A PERSONAL VISION

There's a serious omission in this discussion: no discussion of truly experimental writers, such as Nobel-laureate Samuel Beckett; Robert Kelly whose "Russian Tales" (in his collection, *Cat Scratch Fever*, McPherson & Company, 1991) are "experiments in telling," based on intuitive responses to a chart of Russian-language roots; Diane Williams with her post-modern broken disjunctions (*Some Sexual Success Stories and Other Stories in Which God Might Choose to Appear*, Grove Weidenfeld, 1992). The authors I used as examples may be unconventional, but they are also widely read — and not just by literary sophisticates. I chose them to emphasize a point: You can explore many possibilities in structure and form and still be entirely accessible.

Still, I won't deny that if you hope to be a popular author and even make money at it, you probably stand a better chance if you can write like Stephen King rather than Virginia Woolf. But I don't believe that's a matter of choice. Most writers create out of a personal vision; we each have a particular way of seeing the world.

I began this piece by telling of a student who kept struggling with traditional form. By trying to fit himself into some arbitrary category, this talented writer was unintentionally denying and deforming his gift. When he broke the "rules" for the first time and told his story as he felt it needed to be told, he produced a remarkable piece of fiction that was promptly accepted by a prestigious journal and nominated for a Pushcart Prize. For a writer in search of voice and form, the best literary traditions to keep in mind may be individual vision, innovation and freedom.

TONY KUSHNER

WITH A LITTLE HELP FROM MY FRIENDS

ANGELS IN AMERICA, PART TWO: PERESTROIKA

"Angels in America," Parts 1 and 2, has taken five years to write, and as the work nears completion I find myself thinking a great deal about the people who have left their traces in these texts. The fiction that artistic labor happens in isolation, and that artistic accomplishment is exclusively the provenance of individual talents, is politically charged and, in my case at least, repudiated by the facts.

While the primary labor on "Angels" has been mine, more than two dozen people have contributed words, ideas and structures to these plays, including actors, directors, audiences, one-night stands, my former lover and many friends. Two in particular, my closest friend, Kimberly T. Flynn ("Perestroika" is dedicated to her), and the man who commissioned "Angels," helped shape it and co-directed the Los Angeles production, Oskar Eustis, have had profound influence. Had I written these plays without the participation of my collaborators, they would be entirely different—would, in fact, never have come to be.

Americans pay high prices for maintaining the Myth of the Individual: we have no system of universal health care, we don't educate our children, we can't pass sane gun-control laws, we hate and fear inevitable processes like aging and death.

Way down, close to the bottom of the list of the evils Individualism visits on our culture is the fact that in the modern era it isn't enough to write; you must also be a Writer and play your part as the protagonist in a cautionary narrative in which you will fail or triumph, be in or out, hot or cold. The rewards can be fantastic; the punishment dismal; it's a zero-sum game, and its guarantor of value, its marker, is that you pretend you play it solo, preserving the myth that you alone are the wellspring of your creativity.

When I started to write these plays I wanted to attempt something of ambition and size even if that meant I might be accused of straying too close to ambition's ugly twin, pretentiousness. Given the bloody opulence of this country's great and terrible history, given its newness and its grand improbability, its artists are bound to be tempted toward large gestures and big embraces, a proclivity de Tocqueville deplored as a national artistic trait more than 150 years ago. Melville, my favorite American writer, strikes inflated, even hysterical chords on occasion. It's the sound of the Individual ballooning, overreaching. We are all children of the "Song of Myself."

Anyone interested in exploring alternatives to Individualism and the political economy it serves, Capitalism, has to be willing to ask hard questions about the ego, both as abstraction and as exemplified in oneself.

Bertolt Brecht, while he was still in Weimar-era Berlin and facing the possibility of participating in a socialist revolution, wrote a series of remarkable short plays, his Lehrstucke, or learning plays. The principal subject of these plays was the painful dismantling, as a revolutionary exigency, of the individual ego. His metaphor for this dismantling is death.

(Brecht, who never tried to hide the dimensions of his own titanic personality, didn't sentimentalize the problems such personalities present, or the process of loss involved in attempting to let go of the richness, and the riches, that accompany such successful self-creation.)

He simultaneously claimed and mocked the identity he'd won for himself, "a great German writer," raising important questions about the means of literary production, challenging the sacrosanctity of the image of the solitary artist and, at the same time, openly, ardently wanting to be recognized as a genius. That he was a genius is inarguably the case. For a man deeply committed to collectivity as an ideal and an achievable political goal, this blazing singularity was a mixed blessing at best and at worst an obstacle to a blending of radical theory and practice.

In the lower-right-hand corner of the title page of many of Brecht's plays you will find, in tiny print, a list of names under the heading collaborators. Sometimes these people contributed little, sometimes a great deal. One cannot help feeling that those who bore those minuscule names, who expended the considerable labor the diminutive typography conceals, have had a bum deal. Many of these collaborators, Ruth Berlau, Elisabeth Hauptmann, Margarete Steffin, were women. In the question of shared intellectual and artistic labor, gender is always an issue.

On the day last spring when the Tony nominations were being handed out, I left the clamorous room at Sardi's thinking gloomily that here was another source of anxiety, another obstacle to getting back to work rewriting "Perestroika." In the building's lobby I was introduced to the producer Elizabeth I. McCann, who said to me: "I've been worried about how you were handling all this till I read that you have an Irish woman in your life. Then I knew you were going to be fine." Ms. McCann was referring to Kimberly T. Flynn. An article in *The New Yorker* last year about "Angels in America" described how certain features of our shared experience dealing with her prolonged health crisis, caused by a serious cab accident several years ago, had a major impact on the plays.

Kimberly and I met in 1978 when I was a student at Columbia and she was a student at Barnard. We share Louisiana childhoods (she is from New Orleans, I grew up in Lake Charles), different but equally complicated, powerful religious traditions and an ambivalence toward those traditions; leftist politics informed by, among other things, liberation struggles (she as a feminist, I as a gay man); and a belief in the effectiveness of activism and the possibility of progress.

From the beginning Kimberly was my teacher. Though largely self-taught, she was more widely read and she helped me understand both Freud and Marx. She introduced me to the writers of the Frankfurt School and their early attempts at synthesizing psychoanalysis and Marxism; and to the German philosopher and critic Walter Benjamin, whose importance for me rests primarily in his introduction into these "scientific" disciplines a Kabbalist-inflected mysticism and a dark, apocalyptic spirituality.

As both writer and talker, Kimberly employs a rich variety of rhetorical strategies and effects, even while expressing deep emotion. She identifies this as an Irish trait; it's evident in O'Neill, Yeats, Beckett. This relationship to language, blended with Jewish and gay versions of the same strategies, is evident in my plays, in the ways my characters speak.

More pessimistic than I, Kimberly is much less afraid to look at the ugliness of the world. She tries to protect herself far less than I do and consequently she sees more. She feels safest, she says, knowing the worst, while most people I know, myself included, would rather be spared and feel safer encircled by a measure of obliviousness.

She is capable of teasing out fundamental concerns from their camouflage of words; at the same time she uses her analysis, her learning, her emotions, her lived experience, to make imaginative leaps, to see the deeper connections between ideas and historical developments. Through her example I learned to trust that such leaps can be made; I learned to admire them, in literature, in theory, in the utterances people make in newspapers. And certainly it was in part her example that made the labor of synthesizing disparate, seemingly unconnected things become for me the process of writing a play.

Since the accident Kimberly has struggled with her health, and I have struggled to help her, sometimes succeeding, sometimes failing. It's always been easier talking about the way in which I used what Kimberly and I lived through to write "Angels," even though I sometimes question the morality of the act (while at the same time considering it unavoidable if I was to write at all), than it has been to acknowledge the intellectual debt. People seem to be more interested in the story of the accident and its aftermath than in the intellectual genealogy, the emotional life being privileged over the intellectual life in the business of making plays, and the two being regarded, incorrectly, as separable.

A great deal of what I understand about health issues comes from what Kimberly has endured and triumphed over and the ways she has articulated those experiences. But "Angels" is more the result of our intellectual friendship than it is autobiography, and her contribution was as teacher, editor, advisor, not muse.

Perhaps other playwrights don't have similar relationships or similar debts; perhaps they have. In a wonderful recent collection of essays on creative partnerships, "Significant Others," edited by Isabelle De Courtivron and Whitney Chadwick, the contributors examine both healthy and deeply unhealthy versions of artistic interdependence in such couples as the Delaunays, Kahlo and Rivera, Hammett and Heliman, and Jasper Johns and Robert Rauschenberg—and in doing so strike forcefully at what the editors call "the myth of solitariness."

Since this myth is all important to our view of artistic work, we have no words for the people to whom we are indebted. I call Oskar Eustis a dramaturg, sometimes a collaborator; but collaborator implies co-authorship and nobody knows what dramaturg implies. "Angels" began in a conversation, real and imaginary, with Oskar. A romantic-ambivalent love for American history and belief in what one of the plays' characters calls "the prospect of some sort of radical democracy spreading outward and growing up" are things Oskar and I share, part of the discussions we had for nearly a year before I started writing Part 1. Oskar continues to be for me, intellectually and emotionally, what the developmental psychologists call "a secure base of attachment"(a phrase I learned from Kimberly).

The play is indebted, too, to writers I've never met. It's ironical that Harold Bloom, in his introduction to "Musical Variations on Jewish Thought" by Olivier Revault D'Allones, provided me with a translation of the Hebrew word for "blessing"—"more life"—which subsequently became key to the heart of "Perestroika." Professor Bloom is also the author of "The Anxiety of Influence," his oedipalization of the history of Western literature, which, when I first encountered it years ago, made me so anxious my analyst suggested I put it away. Recently I had the chance to meet Professor Bloom and, guilty over my appropriation of "more life," I fled from the encounter as one of Freud's "Totem and Taboo" tribesmen might flee from a meeting with that primal father, the one with the big knife. (I cite Professor Bloom as the source of the idea in the published script.)

Guilt, of course, plays a part in this confessional account; and I want the people who helped me make these plays to be identified because their labor was consequential. Many important names have not been mentioned, lest this begin to sound like a thank-you note or, worse, an acceptance speech. I have been blessed with remarkable comrades and collaborators; together we organize the world for ourselves, or at least we organize our understanding of it; we reflect it, refract it, criticize it, grieve over its savagery, and help one another to discern, amidst the gathering dark, paths of resistance, pockets of peace and places from whence hope may be plausibly expected.

Marx was right: the smallest divisible human unit is two people, not one; one is a fiction. From such nets of souls societies, the social world, human life spring. And also plays.

JOSIP NOVAKOVICH

CRISS-CROSSED WITH STORIES

HUNGRY MIND REVIEW

I began to write stories in the States out of nostalgia. I had dodged the Yugoslav federal army and could not go home. Even before I left my town, Daruvar, Croatia, at the age of nineteen, my home had changed so much that I could feel exiled while still living in it. But I could not acknowledge yet that the vanishing of the things that had made up the world of my youth somehow created a void in me, a phantom of alienation, as though my limbs had been severed and my nerves still re-created their aura.

When I got to the States, however, I could give a physical expression to this alienation: now there was an ocean, two seas, and nine mountain ranges between me and my town. I had become a certified alien, with an alien registration number (green card), and therefore, though a young man of twenty-two, I could torture people around me with the stories of a time and place when I was not an alien: the backyard where I had grown up in relentless play. (I had started school a year later than I was supposed to — I was nearly eight — because I could not stop playing in the yard.)

Now, the yard and the street outside, the town, the people — I could keep them alive only if I remembered them and communicated with them. I wrote, a letter a day, sometimes a dozen pages, and in return, if I was lucky, I'd get a postcard. That did little for my sense of regaining my homeland: those letters flew away, dissipating my thoughts and longings, and not even a house of cards stayed with me but only a white wall in front of my desk and white paper on the desk. An American friend wondered why I did not put up any pictures on the wall in my room; I thought I would put up a map of the world, but somehow, I did not have enough will for such an action, which would be contained in my room. With letters I had at least an illusion that I was reaching beyond the ocean and plugging my spirit into my native soil, through the bit of a tree—the page—that contained the traces of roots sucking juices of a fertile black soil. Perhaps I did not think like that then, but I do now, remembering how I began to write stories.

When only postcards came back, in flimsy undeveloped handwritings—young men writing like children because they did not love writing—I thought I might just as well give up on the lousy lot of my friends and brothers. But by then I was addicted to remembering through writing, and so I wrote to the wall in front of me, almost a wall of wailing. I described the backyard and the garden of my childhood—the tilting brick wall on the western edge, the clogmaking workshop with a pipe spitting sawdust against the wall, the creaking frog pond, the two dozen humming beehives, the warbling cool alley of grapevines, the smoking garbage dump at the bottom of the garden (there was no garbage collection in our town so we dealt with it at home) where stray cats tiptoed and licked broken eggshells. It took me a hundred pages of describing and remembering, and I was not done. I realized that those bricks in the walls I remembered, each one, when removed, opened a view, a view that excited me with the sorrow of not being there.

Although I had rushed away from my home to go to the promised land of freedom and technological wonders, America, now realizing that waxed supermarket tomatoes did not taste nearly as good as the tomatoes from my childhood garden, I began to strive to get—through my imagination—back to the home that I was prohibited from visiting; I thought that the military would jail me. (Draft dodging was common among Croats, so that when the war with Serbia started, Croats were not prepared, unlike Serbs, most of whom loved the army.)

That I did not strive to go back to the current Croatia but to some edenized childhood home strikes me as a quintessentially exile type of maneuver. I reverted to a stage of near infancy, seeking some kind of security, and the only road back was memory. So, because of memory I became a writer — if I remember correctly. Or, because of nostalgia? Of course, if it had not been for memories, I would have had no nostalgia. Or if it had not been for nostalgia, I would not have remembered so much.

Perhaps if my recall had been sharper, I would have been glad to be out of a muddy Croatian town for good. But since I could not exactly remember the features of the beeches and walnut trees I had climbed (I could not recall knife cuts in the bark, merciless lovers carving out their initials and hearts and arrows), and since I could not recall the furious sounds of quarrels and insults, and the quiet jealousies and hatreds among Serbs and Croats — I strove to behold the town so ferociously, punching holes in the pages on my manual typewriter.

Perhaps I remembered the hometown out of resentment just as much as out of love, out of fear as much as out of pride. Perhaps I wanted somehow to annihilate the town through satire and sarcasm, or raise it, through humor, for I believed that playing with my memories the way I used to play with sawdust, I could laugh and enjoy. The town would not be a threatening but a droll place, the type now and then made into movies, particularly Czech movies, in which a spirit of drunken benevolence makes you giggle. (Our town was, and still is, the center of the Czech minorities in Croatia.) Anyway, from the incomplete memory I created my hometown "as I remembered it," or chose to remember it.

Now it's clear just how incompletely I remembered it, now that my best childhood friend joined a band of chetniks to shell our town from the surrounding hills. Here's how I recalled him years ago in a story: "I invited Danko to the sawdust, where we played dead, burying each other. In summers we knocked down greenskinned walnuts, and smashed them open with pebbles, as though cracking skulls, and indeed, out came little brain hemispheres. We peeled off thin walnut skins from the little brains and chewed the sweet meat, feeling as unfettered as cavemen." While writing this, I thought I was writing something quaint, but now that the friend, as an adult, has probably cracked real skulls,

I see the unquaint side with which I had not been fully acquainted: the aggression. I had remembered the spirit of the experience incompletely (or did not understand what I remembered), yet for that incompleteness, something unsaid, perhaps at the time ineffable, remained, intrigued me, made me marvel — and write.

A better example of how an incomplete memory generated my imagination: when my father was dying, my brother called me to his side. By the time I got to the deathbed, I do not think that my father was conscious anymore. A trickle of bloody foam was sliding down his chin, from the corner of his mouth. My brother had witnessed most of the stages of father's death. However, it was I — not he — who wrote the story of father's death, some seventy pages long. Then later I wrote a novel about a man who fails to die, just as I supposed my father's death was incomplete to me.

So, from my experience (no doubt it works differently for different people) — I think that the incomplete memory, or the memory of an experience not fathomed, provides the strongest impetus to imagine, invent, mold, create. It's the moments just missed that drive you crazy, crazy to live in an imaginary past.

That dwelling-in-the-past-narrowly-missed is by no means unique to me: it is common in Croatia and Serbia and the Balkans in general. Homer narrated past enmities between two continents, and six hundred years after the embellished events in his memories, Greece and Persia were at war; perhaps the poetic memories contributed to the war? Similarly, Serbs narrated and eulogized the Kosovo battle of 1389, in which they had narrowly missed a victory over Turks: with regret spun around defeat, many legends arose, and now, almost exactly six hundred years later, rather than the beautiful oral epic tradition, we have reports of Serbs slaying and raping Muslims ("Turks"), somehow "revising" the memory of the Kosovo defeat. And Croats, too, out of vague memories of kingdoms past, have sought independence at all costs, creating a new country, perhaps. Memories do lead to creation — but equally, to destruction.

I can't attribute any colossal consequences — constructive or destructive — to my storytelling, but I hope that I should be at peace with the town of my youth, so that there should be no need to go back and change and "revise" and "improve" the past. But it is clear to me, now, that in my writing my town has been mostly imagined. It is my town, criss-crossed not with streets but with stories. Such is the generative force of memory lapses.

ADRIENNE RICH

SOMEONE IS WRITING A POEM

WHAT IS FOUND THERE:
NOTEBOOKS ON
POETRY AND POLITICS

The society whose modernization has reached the stage of integrated spectacle is characterized by the combined effect of five principal factors: incessant technological renewal, integration of state and economy, generalized secrecy, unanswerable lies, and eternal present.

The spectator is simply supposed to know nothing and deserves nothing. Those who are watching to see what happens next will never act and such must be the spectator's condition.

—Guy Debord

In a political culture of managed spectacles and passive spectators, poetry appears as a rift, a peculiar lapse, in the prevailing mode. The reading of a poem, a poetry reading, is not a spectacle, nor can it be passively received. It's an exchange of electrical currents through language—that daily, mundane, abused, and ill-prized medium, that instrument of deception and revelation, that material thing, that knife, rag, boat, spoon/reed become pipe/tree trunk become drum/mud become clay flute/conch shell become summons to freedom/old trousers and petticoats become iconography in appliqué/rubber bands stretched around a box become lyre. Diane Glancy: *Poetry uses the hub of a torque converter for a jello mold.* I once saw, in a Chautauqua vaudeville, a man who made recognizably tonal music by manipulating a variety of sizes of wooden spoons with his astonishing fingers. Take that old, material utensil, language, found all about you, blank with familiarity, smeared with daily use, and make it into something that means more than it says. What poetry is made of is so old, so familiar, that it's easy to forget that it's not just the words, but polyrhythmic sounds, speech in its first endeavors (every poem breaks a silence that had to be overcome), prismatic meanings lit by each others' light, stained by each others' shadows. In the wash of poetry the old, beaten, worn stones of language take on colors that disappear when you sieve them up out of the streambed and try to sort them out.

And all this has to travel from the nervous system of the poet, preverbal, to the nervous system of the one who listens, who reads, the active participant without whom the poem is never finished.

I can't write a poem to manipulate you; it will not succeed. Perhaps you have read such poems and decided you don't care for poetry; something turned you away. I can't write a poem from dishonest motives; it will betray its shoddy provenance, like an ill-made tool, a scissors, a drill, it will not serve its purpose, it will come apart in your hands at the point of stress. I can't write a poem simply from good intentions, wanting to set things right, make it all better; the energy will leak out of it, it will end by meaning less than it says.

I can't write a poem that transcends my own limits, though poetry has often pushed me beyond old horizons, and writing a poem has shown me how far out a part of me was walking beyond the rest. I can expect a reader to feel my limits as I cannot, in terms of her or his own landscape, to ask: *But what has this to do with me? Do I exist in this poem?* And this is not a simple or naive question. We go to poetry because we believe it has something to do with us. We also go to poetry to receive the experience of the *not me*, enter a field of vision we could not otherwise apprehend.

Someone writing a poem believes in a reader, in readers, of that poem. The "who" of that reader quivers like a jellyfish. Self-reference is always possible: that my "I" is a universal "we," that the reader is my clone. That sending letters to myself is enough for attention to be paid. That my chip of mirror contains the world.

But most often someone writing a poem believes in, depends on, a delicate, vibrating range of difference, that an "I" can become a "we" without extinguishing others, that a partly common language exists to which strangers can bring their own heartbeat, memories, images. A language that itself has learned from the heartbeat, memories, images of strangers.

Spectacles controlled and designed to manipulate mass opinion, mass emotions depend increasingly on the ownership of vast and expensive technologies and on the physical distance of the spectators from the spectacle. (The bombing of Baghdad, the studios where competing camera shots were selected and edited and juxtaposed to project via satellite dazzling images of a clean, nonbloody war.) I'm not claiming any kind of purity for poetry, only its own particular way of being. But it's notable that the making of and participation in poetry is so independent of high technology. A good sound system at a reading is of course a great advantage. Poetry readings can now be heard on tape, radio, recorded on video. But poetry would get lost in an immense technological performance scene. What poetry can give has to be given through language and voice, not through massive effects of lighting, sound, superimposed film images, nor as a mere adjunct to spectacle.

I need to make a crucial distinction here. The means of high technology are, as the poet Luis J. Rodriguez has said of the microchip, "surrounded by social relations and power mechanisms which arose out of another time, another period; . . . [they are] imprisoned by capitalism." The spectacles produced by these means carry the messages of those social relations and power mechanisms: that our conditions are inevitable, that randomness prevails, that the only possible response is passive absorption and identification.

But there is a different kind of performance at the heart of the renascence of poetry as an oral art—the art of the griot, performed in alliance with music and dance, to evoke and catalyze a community or communities against passivity and victimization, to recall people to their spiritual and historic sources. Such art, here and now, does not and cannot depend on huge economic and technical resources, though in a different system of social relations it might well draw upon highly sophisticated technologies for its own ends without becoming dominated by them.

Someone is writing a poem. Words are being set down in a force field. It's as if the words themselves have magnetic charges; they veer together or in polarity, they swerve against each other. Part of the force field, the charge, is the working history of the words themselves, how someone has known them, used them, doubted and relied on them in a life. Part of the movement among the words belongs to sound — the guttural, the liquid, the choppy, the drawn-out, the breathy, the visceral, the downlight. The theater of any poem is a collection of decisions about space and time — how are these words to lie on the page, with what pauses, what headlong motion, what phrasing, how can they meet the breath of the someone who comes along to read them? And in part the field is charged by the way images swim into the brain through written language: swan, kettle, icicle, ashes, scab, tamarack, tractor, veil, slime, teeth, freckle.

Lynn Emanuel writes of a nuclear-bomb test watched on television in the Nevada desert by a single mother and daughter living on the edge in a motel:

THE PLANET KRYPTON

Outside the window the McGill smelter
sent a red dust down on the smoking yards of copper,
on the railroad tracks' frayed ends disappeared
into the congestion of the afternoon. Ely lay dull

and scuffed: a miner's boot toe worn away and dim,
while my mother knelt before the Philco to coax
the detonation from the static. From the Las Vegas
Tonapah Artillery and Gunnery Range the sound

of the atom bomb came biting like a swarm
of bees. We sat in the hot Nevada dark, delighted,
when the switch was tripped and the bomb hoisted
up its silky, hooded, glittering, uncoiling length;

it hissed and spit, it sizzled like a poker in a toddy.
The bomb was no mind and all body; it sent a fire
of static down the spine. In the dark it glowed like the coils
of an electric stove. It stripped every leaf from every

branch until a willow by a creek was a bouquet
of switches resinous, naked, flexible, and fine.
Bathed in the light of KDWN, Las Vegas,
my crouched mother looked radioactive, swampy,

glaucous, like something from the Planet Krypton.
In the suave, brilliant wattage of the bomb, we were
not poor. In the atom's fizz and pop we heard possibility
uncorked. Taffeta wraps whispered on davenports.

A new planet bloomed above us; in its light
the stumps of cut pine gleamed like dinner plates.
The world was beginning all over again, fresh and hot;
we could have anything we wanted.

In the suave, brilliant wattage of the bomb, we were/not poor. This,
you could say, is the political core of the poem, the "meaning"
without which it could not exist. All that the bomb was meant to
mean, as spectacle of power promising limitless possibilities to
the powerless, all the falseness of its promise, the original devas-
tation of two cities, the ongoing fallout into local communities,
reservations — all the way to the Pacific Islands — this is the driving impulse of the poem, the energy it rides. Yet all this would
be mere "message" and forgettable without the poem's visual
fury, its extraordinary leaps of sound and image: *Ely lay dull/
and scuffed: a miner's boot toe worn away and dim. . . . Taffeta wraps
whispered on davenports.* The Planet Krypton is Superman's
planet, falling apart, the bits of rubble it flings to Earth danger-

ous to the hero; Earth has become its own Planet Krypton—auto-toxic.

At a certain point, a woman, writing this poem, has had to reckon the power of poetry as distinct from the power of the nuclear bomb, of the radioactive lesions of her planet, the power of poverty to reduce people to spectators of distantly conjured events. She can't remain a spectactor, hypnotized by the gorgeousness of a destructive force launched far beyond her control. She can feel the old primary appetites for destruction and creation within her; she chooses for creation and for language. But to do this she has to see clearly—and to make visible—how destructive power once seemed to serve her needs, how the bomb's *silky, hooded, glittering, uncoiling length* might enthrall a mother and daughter as they watched, two marginal women, clinging to the edges of a speck in the desert. Her handling of that need, that destructiveness, in language, is how she takes on her true power.

BONNIE FRIEDMAN

YOUR MOTHER'S PASSIONS, YOUR SISTER'S WOES: WRITING ABOUT THE LIVING

WRITING PAST DARK

For centuries Dedalus has represented the type of the artist-scientist: that curiously disinterested, almost diabolic human phenomenon, beyond the normal bounds of social judgment, dedicated to the morals not of his time but of his art.

—Joseph Campbell

The best stories I know I must not tell. One of them concerns my cousin Robert. I haven't seen him in years. As children we went to the same bungalow colony, and amid the Creamsicle and lemon summer houses and oceans of hot, clipped grass, there was simply the sense that there was something strange about Robert (this is not his real name).

He was, I think, prone to frantic, unappeasable tantrums when he should have been too old for them, and he wandered into the girls' changing room with his pants unzipped, so that now the smell of frilled rubber bathing caps and mildewed carpeting always calls to mind for me that ribbon of pink flesh, a bald human bookmark soon squashed and hidden—but not before Robert absorbed our horror, his big eyes staring.

My mother remembers him earlier, as a very little boy strolling down to the lake in Mount Liberty, fat, with a yeasty white belly and bare feet, a red sand pail overturned on his head.

"He looked so funny," my mother says, "with that bucket down over his head."

"Maybe he was pretending to be a soldier, and the bucket was his helmet."

"No-o," she says, pondering. "I don't think it was that. The bucket was too low for that. It was right down over his face."

And now recently a different cousin, Charlotte, ran into Robert. They had a long talk. He is a nice-looking young man with dark hair, and he is no longer fat. "He told me," she says, "that it sometimes takes four or five hours to leave the house. He will look in the mirror and see something about his appearance that bothers him, and he will have to change it. He washes his hair over and over so he can blow-dry it correctly. He buttons and unbuttons the top button of his shirt."

"Five hours?" I say. "That's an exaggeration."

"No, I don't think so. If you met him, I'm sure you'd think it was true."

She can't tell me anything else about him, though, because in fact he swore her to silence.

"Oh, come on," I say.

She shakes her head. "I shouldn't have told you this much. Still, if you'd met him—there is just something so odd about him . . ."

Robert lives on disability at an undisclosed address in Ocean City—he won't tell his parents where. If I described his brittle, caustic mother, his jumpy brother, his reclusive father, you could probably see how all their lives have been shaped by Robert, and how his life has been shaped by theirs.

This man's life, everything about him, is the family secret. And I want to write about it.

Similarly, I'd like to write about the woman who lived down the hall from us in apartment 5B when I was growing up. Her parents forbade her to marry the man she loved because he wasn't a Jew.

"What was he?" I asked.

"He was in fact a very religious man. Kept kosher, kept his head covered." My mother shrugged. "He *was* Jewish, but for Mrs. Landau nobody was good enough. She told Stella if she married him, forget it. She wouldn't have anything to do with her."

Stella broke off the engagement and took a long trip around the world, but had to come home early because she'd contracted a disease. One of the symptoms of this disease was that she could not walk. Another was that her stomach was so weak she could hardly eat. She lay down in her parents' apartment, and her mother nursed her for month after month.

I was in that apartment. It was in those days a murky place with two tiny bedrooms that funneled into a kitchenette. A dog we called "the pickle dog" because of its yellow-green fur seemed to decompose on the linoleum. The father, a man with a stiff broad upper body like a door, sat at a table mutely reading a newspaper. The mother, in lumpy dark wool clothes she'd sewn herself, clothes so thick it seemed a whole box of pins could disappear inside, stirred the pot of saltless spinach soup that always simmered, releasing a pervasive vegetable scent. And Stella drowsed in one of the bedrooms, letting herself be nursed.

Of course she was brought from doctor to doctor as the seasons passed. A fortune was spent. Her tests all turned up normal. At last it was decided she must have been infected by a rare tropical virus no American doctor could recognize. Around this time Stella got up, recovered her health, and married the man she loved. Her mother, true to her word, wouldn't see her. She hung up when the daughter phoned. In the elevator she merely blinked, one long stony blink, if a neighbor asked about Stella. At last, after three years, the mother admitted defeat, and took the train to Mount Kisco to visit the grandson whose face she'd never seen.

This second story is easier to tell because the whole family has moved away, and because it has a happy, almost fairy-talish end. It existed for me first *as* a story—my mother told it—and it is important to me because it reminds me of girlhoods that happened all over the Bronx, fierce romances between mothers and daughters in which a husband could only be a betrayal. I become more comprehensible to myself when I hear these stories; they belong to me, too.

The first story, though, which I've sketched despite a certain heartsick guilt, matters to me more. The man himself is alone, and writing about him feels like paying attention the way Willy Loman's wife asks when she says, "Attention must be paid." Also, our parents are still in touch; our own lives still feel close. I cannot fall under the illusion that because I remember this man from long ago I understand him. At family gatherings he hovers at the edge of awareness, the man who is absent. I want to write my way into him. I want to fill him up with my words. I want to see him by pouring my words into him, the way an iodine dye reveals a system of veins.

The most difficult lives to write about — and the ones that draw us most — are full of this same mystery and familiarity. They are the ones where there is the greatest chance people involved will read it and, despite disguises, recognize themselves. These are the lives that brush against ours with a prickly closeness — like someone standing right behind us, someone staring at us, about to touch us, so that the hair on our neck rises instinctively. We want to stop them. We want to see them.

Is it wrong to write about the living?

"If you want to be a writer, somewhere along the line you're going to have to hurt somebody. And when that time comes, you go ahead and do it," Charles McGrath said when he was an editor at *The New Yorker*. "If you can't or don't want to tell that truth, you may as well stop now and save yourself a lot of hardship and pain."

What sort of morality is this? That your own work is more important than someone else's suffering? That your own particular art is more important than your aunt or neighbor? And what if the writing is poor? What if the pain caused is just too intense for the person written about to bear?

A novelist wrote a withering account of her recent marriage. Soon after the book came out, the author's ex-husband killed himself. Was she correct to write that novel?

Say yes, and you may be advocating idolatry.

"The chief characteristic of an idol," Cynthia Ozick says, "is that it is a system sufficient to itself . . . It is indifferent to the world and to humanity . . . That dead matter will rule the quick is the single law of idolatry." If the story of your neighbor's life is more important than your neighbor herself, if the fossil of your neighbor's life, cast by the pressure of granite years, is more important than the actual person desperately trying to manage on the other side of the wall, then Art is a kind of god. It rises lustrous as some golden calf that shudders and sweats in firelight but by day remains aloof.

It is a sin to embarrass, the cantor of my girlhood synagogue taught. It makes blood surge to the victim's face, a rush of blood like a mini-death. God Himself proclaims, "None of you shall come near anyone of his own flesh to uncover nakedness." Leviticus lists all the various family relationships one must not violate by disclosure, and culminates with, "All who do any of these abhorrent things—such people shall be cut off from their people."

Cut off. This is alarming because along with forbidding incest, the rule against uncovering nakedness may mean do not write about what goes on behind closed doors, even if you've grown up behind them.

But my point is not that we should not write about the living. I bring up the Bible in order to acknowledge the deep-rooted nature of the taboo, why it can strike with such paralyzing strength.

Taboo, Freud points out, is a Polynesian word. Its meaning "branches off into two opposite directions. On the one hand it means to us, sacred, consecrated: but on the other hand it means, uncanny, dangerous, forbidden, and unclean."

Something harlequin, mixed, ambiguous, alloyed, hides in our twin desire and aversion to write about the living. It is not only the taboo person that we want to protect. We stretch out our hand to point, yet instantly snatch it back as if we saw it withered—like the wicked witch's feet gnarled up and then withdrawn when the beautiful ruby slippers are removed, like a skeletal finger in a horror movie: the flesh burnt off and the deeper human truth revealed.

The taboo has primal origins. It is, to some extent, implicit in being civilized. As we learn to talk we learn not to say what we see if it might cause hurt. Do not stare darling. Do not point. He doesn't walk funny. You mustn't say that. We'll discuss it when we get home.

But at home, too, certain silences prevail. That slammed door? We have learned not to ask. That dark look? That whiff, perhaps, of alcoholic breath? We have learned to say nothing, even to ourselves. It is as if the unsaid had not occurred, and the less it is referred to, the more invisible it becomes until at last it vanishes into the texture of ordinary interaction like the mesh everything is woven on: all you see are the tidy stitches, the lovely picture they form.

The force of the forbidden draws us. We want its power. We want to use it for our work. We also long to understand the unarticulated, our own most potent reality not yet structured by words. For in fact the secrets we most want to understand are not secrets at all; they are nothing hidden so much as not yet discovered. They are what has been there all along, not furtively denied so much as never consciously noticed.

Taboo has two hands; it points opposite ways. It is like—to use another Oz image—the scarecrow at the crossroads, who by knotting himself calls attention to himself. He wishes to be freed. He wishes to be made whole, or rather *real*—that utmost desire of childhood. Children identify with their own toys; we all felt what it is to be a prop, an adjunct, a creature with eyes converted to flat buttons, and a mouth that is pretty, but sewn.

And now the page beckons.

Thin as the layer of silver that makes a mirror reflect, it urges, Set down here what you saw, and you will see it as never before.

And so will all the world.

Lucille, a friend of mine, told me the story of the novelist's ex-husband. She told the story irritably, swinging her crossed leg. It suggested something, I think, that she wanted to believe and yet could not. And so she found it necessary to proceed without belief.

She had returned to writing after a long, uneasy time away, a time spent traveling, and editing a business journal she did not much care about, and gazing out the window at the other mothers her age advancing down the street behind silvery high-tech strollers.

Now that she was writing again, she took her work more seriously, and the more seriously she took it, the more she wrote about her family. She was in her late twenties and then her early thirties. She had a husband and a child, and she bore down on her writing as if it were a shovel stuck in the frozen ground that she must press on with all her might. She hung the weight of her whole life upon her words, honing them, honing them, until she broke the surface and brought up diamonds.

She was writing about being Asian-American, the daughter of immigrant parents. In one story a mother who remains in slippers and a robe all day insists her daughter practice the violin many hours each evening, although the girl now despises the instrument. Both mother and daughter seem to fear that without the violin, the girl will be nothing. Another story begins with a father removing his dentures. Quite precisely we are told the exact pulpy look of the father's mouth when he takes out the false teeth. The description is not gratuitous. It is essential to the story, which happens to end up underscoring the wisdom of the father, which the adolescent daughter scorned. Still, when the story appeared in print, Lucille's father came to her.

He let her know that her writing about him pained him sometimes. He did not understand what he had done to her that she was so angry. He spoke for her mother, saying she also was disturbed. Please do not write about us anymore, he asked.

If my own father said this to me, I would feel in an absolute cauldron of guilt. My fantasies have always been to take lavish care of my parents as they grow older, and to make them proud of me. But could I give up writing about them if they asked?

Lucille refused. She loved her parents, but would not silence herself for them. If she could not write about what was most central to her, she told me later, she could not write at all. And yet, when she did write about them now, she said, she felt "like a ghoul."

My friend Regi set to writing essays. "Have you noticed," she inquired, "how if you let yourself write only nice things about people it ends up sounding like the kind of speech people give at a graveside? A eulogy, I mean? And how your writing really springs to life when you write something that, if they read it, they would *just die*?"

Again there is the suspicion that, in some sense, what's dead feeds on what's living, as if you are in Dr. Frankenstein's remote fortress lab, where your own mother, for instance, is strapped to one table and your blank book to the other. Again there is a strange confusion between what deserves to breathe and what deserves to be buried: character "assassinations" that violate the souls of the living, truths so deeply interred in living people's bodies that these people come to resemble figures of wax, yellowish, nerveless, like someone molded out of calluses, as if the artificial person — the one who maintains a heavy fraudulence, stifling beneath a fog of perfume the most necessary truths — has become in herself a squat golden god, a Madame Tussaud effigy, roughed and lipsticked and propped in a corner, and you can imagine sticking pins in without causing pain. Death drifts from such a person, from the dry whole-wheat toast and the grapefruit halves, the puzzled frown at what nice people don't say, at what she herself refuses, it seems, to understand, so that it is tempting to see this mountainous pale figure as unfeeling, inert, molten candlestuff, laminated shut.

It is as if, in fact, the painful truth were a pin which the other person — one's mother, for instance — has swallowed deep within her, beneath layers and layers of herself. This hidden shard of truth is rigid as a stalactite, and one must force her to surrender it, opening her jaws and prizing it loose, because you need it to cut your own self free. It is as if the truth she's swallowed belongs to you, and as long as she denies what you've both seen, you cannot belong entirely to yourself; you are incredible, unreal, a magic slate whose sheet is lifted up again and again. ("I never, for a minute, resented you when you were a child." "Your sister adored you, always." "You gave my whole life meaning." "I did not send you away because I wanted to be rid of you. I only wanted you to be happy." Some examples of rubbery denial.) In later years, even if you bear down on your magic slate with empathic force, pressing into the thick dark wax under the film — like writing into a plum of your own hand, trying to force the body to register its own experience — it doesn't matter. Out of habit, the gray film lifts. One detaches from what one felt, mistrusting it. Blankness returns.

We need confirmation from outside. We need to be seen and

read aloud as if we were books in another's hands: our own ghostly thoughts set striding. How else can we become real? We reach toward the bones in our mother's ears, the malleus, incus, and stapes, small as thorns. We reach toward the spine, wanting its solidity. Our sword in the stone grows straight down through our parents. They are right to regard us with alarm.

My mother clipped my fingernails and burnt them over the gas stove when I was a child. I still recall the acrid smell, and the curling, blackening. She didn't want anyone to find my nails and make voodoo out of them. My friend Sandra in high school kept a clear medicine bottle of her nail clippings by her bed. There it was, a little walled place crawling with waxy slivers, the whitish nails scaling the vial, curling and tumbling among themselves, a bevy of moons, a packed cramped cell teeming with Sandra's body — she didn't want to throw them out perhaps for the same reason my mother didn't throw mine out, a terror of enemies, a lust to keep herself for herself and not to release even her debris into the world.

Freud describes a "taboo patient" who "adopted the avoidance of writing down her name for fear it might get into somebody's hands who thus would come into possession of a piece of her personality. In her frenzied faithfulness, which she needed to protect herself against the temptations of her phantasy, she had created for herself the commandment, 'not to give away anything of her personality.' To this belonged first of all her name, then by further application her handwriting, so that she finally gave up writing."

We must keep hold of our bodies because of what they might do if let loose. We must hoard our scraps of paper, and our scraps of nail, and transform our biting teeth into something a fairy can claim by setting them under our sleeping heads — letting our mothers have our teeth for the price of a candy, redeeming our bones for a dime, lying at our utmost vulnerable with the loose incisor beneath us so that, once we are dead to life, a switch can occur, and money and sweetness can console for the loss of our aggressive edge. It is an ancient belief: the body, sparked with passions, prison of all errant thoughts, is dangerous when free. It is, symbolically, the unconscious unchained.

Split from rational control, it will do what it wants, betraying us.

Even what's dead of ours has a kind of life. And in our lives we experience patches of death, whole nights and days when we feel stuffed with sawdust, made of soaked skin like bandages, puffy, mummyish, fluttering off the frame. We die instead of feel. We worry our truths will kill. If we are mute, and bottle them up, perhaps they will kill only us.

So, who is the unfeeling wax figure? Who is the figure of Yellow Death? Is it the person who maintains a heavy fraudulence, or is it really one's own self? The emotionally deadened person seems calloused, insensate, reminiscent of drained wax bottles, the wax candy-soda bottles of childhood. We used to drink the sweet liquid—blue, red, green—then chew the loaf of wax: it was curious, like chewing one's own anesthetized mouth after the dentist, one's own mouth bereft of sensation, a big bloated fascinating thing like a sort of rubber goiter blooming off one's face, one's face pulled into an elastic, Silly Putty mockery of itself, a gargoyle of itself, the way my sister used to pull my face between viselike fingers, giving me a *kanip*, a savage double-pinch, while cooing, "Am I giving you conniptions?"—showing love while inflicting pain. Confusion smothered my feelings about her, and her true emotion remained invisible to me.

Which one of us was the figure who does not feel? Whose is the inert body one would force into consciousness? In writing about the living, aren't we trying to access something living in us, living incognito, interred, resisted, half-formed, sharp as a fang?

"I do not know what I have done to you that you are so angry at me," Lucille's father said.

His comment struck her as naive. This was just something she'd written. She was just using her material. And yet she would not surrender this material even for love. Without it—like the daughter with the violin—she feared she would be nothing.

Frankenstein, Mary Shelley's myth about bringing the dead to life, is in fact a parable about sacrificing family for the sake of artistic ambition. It reads like a transcript of our fears.

Young Victor Frankenstein goes far away. There's something

he wants to know: the secret "of life." What exactly is the spark that makes creatures live? Excited by the rather prurient idea that scientists "penetrated into the recesses of nature and show how she works in her hiding-places," he stalks the graveyard; he dwells in the charnel-house. Taboo means nothing to him.

"My attention was fixed upon every object the most insupportable to the delicacy of human feeling," he says. "I saw how the fine form of man was degraded and wasted; I beheld the corruption of death succeed to the blooming cheek of life."

Only by examining what others shrink from — by viewing people's degradation and corruption, that is — can he hope to make his great discovery.

And yet his avowed aim is not to disparage, but rather to "pour a torrent of light on our dark world," much as James Joyce's artist hero, Dedalus, might have put it — as if art were a drenching sun; as if he hoped to open a deluge of illumination.

To do his work, Frankenstein must ignore his family. When he is in touch with them, when he so much as writes them a letter, he cannot go on. Being in touch with them puts him in touch with his own natural sense of horror, and he realizes what in fact his hands have been touching: things meant by all spiritual authority to be let rest underground.

So Frankenstein turns a deaf ear to his family, their anxious questions and pleas. "I knew well therefore what would be my father's feeling," he says, "but I could not tear my thoughts from my employment, loathsome in itself, but which had taken an irresistible hold of my imagination. I wished, as it were, to procrastinate all that related to my feelings of affection until the great object, which swallowed up every habit of my nature, should be completed."

How closely this mirrors the confession a writer once made to me! She had just published a novel based on her life and the lives of people she was close to, when she wrote this: "I realized very early on that if I was going to be worrying about what my parents or husband's ex-wife or stepchildren were going to think, if I wasn't going to be free to write the best book I could, whatever that meant in terms of possible hurt to people I was involved with, then I simply could not write that novel. So I shelved all the worries, figuring I'd deal with them later."

In Shelley's tale, which ends in such famous catastrophe, the artist's decision to ignore his family is not merely part of the problem; it is the problem. The author has Dr. Frankenstein proclaim, "If this law was always observed; if no man allowed any pursuit whatsoever to interfere with the tranquillity of his domestic affections, Greece had not been enslaved, Caesar would have spared his country . . . and the empires of Mexico and Peru had not been destroyed."

For as soon as Frankenstein has the knowledge he wants, he yearns to "author" (Shelley's word) fresh life. He cuts apart dead people, steals pieces, stitches these together, and then bestows the spark that makes his creature live. In other words, Frankenstein performs a physical analogue, a sort of physical enactment of imaginative writing. His project involves anatomical secrets; writers' work involves historical and psychological secrets. His work requires exhuming bodies; writers' work requires unburying events and emotions which have been suppressed. In both cases real people become mere material for the creator's ends.

And what happens when the work is done?

The instant Frankenstein's creature opens its eyes, its "author" is aghast. "The beauty of the dream vanished, and breathless horror and disgust filled my heart." Appalled, the doctor flees.

Why? Why isn't he delighted by his success? Why doesn't he think, okay, the creature's not so great to look at. In fact, it's ugly. But what's some yellow skin and black lips compared to what I've just accomplished? I made this thing live!

It's as if at last all the horror he's been suppressing is released. Or rather, it's as if all the emotions he repressed while working were actually going into his creation, which he now despises. The monster is the unconscious incarnate. It is the unconscious with hands and feet.

It stalks his "author" to his hometown. Here are the people Frankenstein always describes in idealized ways. For instance, there is Elizabeth, who his parents adopted when he was five, ending his status as his parents' only child and "idol." Elizabeth became his mother's favorite, and on her deathbed his mother extracted a promise that Frankenstein would marry her. Yet Frankenstein reports, "Everyone loved Elizabeth . . . Harmony was the soul of our companionship, and the diversity and contrast that subsisted in our characters drew us nearer together." Similarly rhapsodic about his general upbringing, he says, "No human being could have passed a happier childhood than myself. My parents were possessed by the very spirit of kindness and indulgence," etc.

At once, the monster slays Frankenstein's angelic youngest brother, and goes on to strangle Frankenstein's highly virtuous best friend. On Frankenstein's wedding night, the "demonaical corpse" seizes Elizabeth, the bride, and chokes her to death. Frankenstein's aged father perishes of grief.

Once finished, the creation is beyond the author's control. It destroys all that he holds dear. When at last the creator himself dies, it is with relief. His agonizing guilt will finally end.

Shelley's story contains, in nightmare form, a writer's phantom fears. The melodrama of it—the thunder crashes, the feverish moonlit rooms—merely reflects the tenor of our repressed anxieties.

Frankenstein reports that he "disturbed, with profane fingers, the tremendous secrets of the human frame"—as if the hand obeyed its own rapacious morality. In fact, the monster's "signature" is strangling—he stifles all his victims, leaving "no sign of any violence except the black mark of fingers on [the] neck."

The beast seems to be body gone wild, the sin of immoral fingers conveyed through the flesh, as if how a thing is made is what it does, and an author's hand will communicate to his or her work all sorts of secret messages, whorling, cross-hatched, gouged inscriptions, willow trees and angels' heads, that it will in turn reveal as it travels through time. There are secrets within secrets that even the writer merely suspects.

I am looking not for objective truth but for emotional truth. I am looking for the way writing about the living feels when we feel its dangers most forcefully, when we wake at 4 A.M. dreading what we have done during the day and what its repercussions will be.

What we feel at 4 A.M. we also feel at 10 A.M. but with this difference: the day casts a sort of scrim before it so that the hunched form that pursues us is diffused, wrapped in haze. At 4 A.M. the light shines straight through, showing the stalker in all its clarity. Better turn and see who it is. Maybe there is something the gnarled, tenacious form is trying to say.

When I was growing up my family had a secret. My sister was fat. It was the only thing you were not allowed to say. In an argument you might say many nasty things, but never this. It would be too painful. It would kill her. She could never forgive you. It was too mean. And yet it was the most obvious thing about her, maybe the most important. It seemed implicated everywhere in her life: who her friends were, whether she came straight home from school or went to the Fordham Road library by herself, and whether she rode the 10 bus or trudged up the long Kingsbridge hill to our house on foot to save the twenty cents for an ice cream, and what that ice cream meant, and how much she spoke at the dinner table, and if you were allowed to interrupt.

It was implicated too somehow in those energetic Saturday afternoons spent whipping up big batches of bread and kolaches from scratch, and in my mother's complaints about the value of the half-dozen fresh white eggs she mixed in, the cupfuls of sifted flour, the butter — melted, "clarified," to a flowing gold, and then worked into the heavy mass of batter in the bowl — what it meant when, vexed by my mother's remarks, and in a tearful fury, she grabbed the bowl and marched down the building corridor and heaved it all — purchased ingredients and afternoon's intent and pleasured labor — down the incinerator. Gone. My mother gazed at me and bit her lip. My sister walked past us and flung shut the bathroom door. We heard her turn the lock, and then, sobbing, wrench apart thick magazines — my mother's *Vogue*, the library's *Cosmopolitan* — and with each sizzling rip it was as if she were tearing flesh. All this had to do somehow with Anita's weight.

Of course in a way there was no need to discuss it. It was what one could not for a moment forget. By not discussing it, though, it was as if one must see Anita but not see her. We saw her and didn't see her, we spoke to her and didn't speak to her, we loved her for who she was and we refused to acknowledge who she was. Are all secrets this obvious? I recall her at a street corner — she had just stepped off the number 10 bus and was walking slowly in her oatmeal cloth coat and molded shoes up the street. She walked like an old woman. Her body was like a heavy, doleful burden she must advance. How bright the pavement was! How slow and steady were her feet!

At writing school I wrote a story about two sisters. One of them was fat. This was the first thing I wrote when I got to writing school, far away from Riverdale, in the scorched Midwest. Everyone was worried that the corn in the fields was burning from the sun's force. Afternoons, it was so hot you could almost smell char in the rare breeze. The skies were as open as plate glass, the color of wheat. I walked around euphoric and dazed. I saw a pig. I thought it was the most exotic thing I'd ever seen. I bought a wooden bowl and a cookbook, but ate frozen fishsticks almost every night. Because I'd never eaten them before, these too seemed exotic. Those first nights, in a small, tight efficiency apartment that looked like a motel and smelled of the vinyl pull-out couch and the new brown and blue rug, my knees locked into the keyhole of the student desk, the air spinning with the grinding of cicadas, a sound I'd never heard before in my life, all I could think about was the Bronx, and being nine, and singing rounds with my sister when we brought her home from Andre Clark Girl Scout Camp.

"My ears are plugged up with my fingers," was the first sentence I wrote there. My second and third were: "My voice sounds muffled and echoey, like singing into a bottle, and the entire time there's a seashell hum in the background and at the end of it, Anna's tiny voice singing my tune before I reach it. It's a round, and if I don't keep my ears shut I get confused and end up singing Anna's part."

Now it strikes me that this first writing had to do with voice, with trying to be deaf to oneself so as not to sound like someone else. At the time, though, I knew just that I wanted to write about Anita. At last, far away, in what seemed like the most alien place although it was the heartland, I turned to her. I assumed she would never read a word I wrote. It was like writing with milk, with invisible ink, in a diary locked with a key I'd swallow.

"Hmm. It doesn't come to much," my writing teacher said, but I knew it had come farther than I'd thought possible. It started in Briarcliff Manor, New York, and ended up on my own doorstep on Johnson Avenue, and in that it had come farther than my writing had ever come before.

Obscurity would swallow these stories, I thought, and so protecting Anita from them did not concern me. If I published them, they would be in journals no one had heard of, under a name that did not yet exist. Actually, though, I thought little of publication. I was always on to something else. I wrote quickly, that first semester, in a room that was innocuous, anonymous. At night I fantasized I was in Alaska, in Tuscaloosa, someplace far. The room was a box with a window under a black sky. You couldn't hear so much as a car whoosh past. I wrote into obscurity; it accepted all I gave. I could write anything, yet what I did write was more and more about the character Anna. And gradually I realized I wanted to write a novel.

The novel I had planned was about disease in a family. My own sister not only was fat, but had developed multiple sclerosis. It was just a tingling in her elbow at first, a pins-and-needles that would not go away, as if just that part of her had fallen asleep and was perpetually in the process of waking up. Pins-and-needles, and then a clumsiness of the hand, and then a drag of the foot. At her wedding she moved stiff as a robot down the aisle in thick white shoes like nurse's shoes, leaning on our parents. Her dress, which my mother chose off the rack at Macy's, was knee-length, so it wouldn't interfere. Anita had asked for no dancing at her wedding because she could not dance. Instead, a man played electronic keyboard, Muzak versions of "We've Only Just Begun" and "Sunrise, Sunset" that were surprisingly pleasant. At one point I noticed Anita sitting by herself. Everyone else was up and mingling, but she could not get to her feet without help. She sat alone, in the middle of the long linen-covered laminated-wood table, her elbow raised awkwardly as she spooned cantaloupe into her mouth while she gazed down at her plate. In a moment I was up and rushing to her, but still that earlier glimpse of her remained.

I wanted my novel also to include scenes that showed in precise detail what this disease did to her body and mind. How could I write about what I saw? It was a shame, the sort you drop your eyes from. You do not stop and point. I wanted to stop and point. I wanted to point so the whole world would see. I did not want the world to drop their eyes from her. I wanted to transcribe the exact creak of her aluminum walker as she approaches my parents' apartment for Friday night supper on the days she's well enough to walk, the exact same corridor she bolted down as a girl, rushing from the incinerator. I wanted to transcribe the exact thump of the rubber-tipped legs of the walker she casts before her, and the precise metallic rasp as she leans on it, and the rough swish of her slippers as she drags her stony feet. One of her feet, twisted perpetually out, must be lifted over the threshold for her. My mother cuts her chicken for her; she can no longer wield a knife. Since Anita spends almost all day alone in her apartment, sitting in the worn gold-velour chair my father gave her, she doesn't have many things to talk about. She tells about reruns of "Mystery!" and "Hawaii Five-O," and her conversation with the man at *Short Story International* when she called to renew her subscription, and about the fact that when she was at City College she took calculus for fun—"for fun, mind you!" she repeats, brandishing the handle of her fork, because, she says, she had a highly organized mind and liked to use it. She eats little. She used to be a great reader—reading was her escape—but now manages only two or three pages a day. Her disease blurs vision in a way glasses can't fix. One day she said to me, "I'm having so much trouble seeing. I need a stronger prescription. Do you think it's possible for grease from your hair to get on your eyes?" When she sits, arms drooped in her lap, she looks hunched. Her body is prone to "accidents"—the reek of urine, her anxious glance: oh, the humilation! I wanted to write it all down.

Why? I wanted to say, simply, this happened. It seemed almost horrible that others did not know, that the world had not responded to it. How did I expect the world to respond? I didn't know. Only, the rest of the world seemed heartless for not knowing the truth of Anita's life. In part, fury made me want to press Anita's story in people's faces. It actually seemed to me that the world could not hear the truth of Anita's life and continue as it had. Something would have to change. And I wanted to challenge God. I had selected an epigram for my unwritten novel. "Should not the Judge of the world deal justly?" — Genesis 18:25.

I thought I wasn't religious, but when I wrote about multiple sclerosis, God appeared. There He was, indicted. The world's beauty had never sent me looking for explanations; it was the botches that suggested God's signature, as if He'd gotten careless blotting His pen, as if, in neglect or rage for some inscrutable reason, He'd left the ink nub to pool darkly on the page. Sometimes my own sister seemed like Frankenstein's monster, and Frankenstein was God, or, if I wrote about her, Frankenstein was me.

In the novel I planned, I wanted to examine not only an older sister's disease, but a younger sister's response. I imagined a plot in which the older sister comes to live with the younger when her body worsens, much as I feared my own sister would come to live with me. To the younger sister I gave many riches: a country house made of a renovated barn, a teaching job at the state university, a baby, and a husband who would be understanding up to a certain point.

The older sister, in my plot, would come to dominate the life of the younger. There would be a bitter scene at supper when the older accused the younger of coldness and selfishness, and a scene in which the younger realized her sister, occupying the bedroom next door, could probably hear her having sex, and there would be a third during which the older sister was jealous of the infant, and complained bitterly about her. Tensions would develop in the younger sister's marriage. A choice would have to be made. Will the younger sacrifice herself for the older, to save the older going into a nursing home? Added to this would be scenes of closeness between the two sisters, occasions of intimacy greater than any friend or even husband could achieve.

It was a dark book I had planned. It made out of my history my future — issues of domination and self-sacrifice had overrun my life with my sister, growing up. Her rages and griefs, the tyrannical hold she could exert over an entire household—all this the page would register, as well as our passionate love for each other. And yet this story seemed too mean to write. Even simply describing the disease seemed heartless.

"M.S. stands for three things," my sister once said at Friday supper. All soup spoons paused in mid-air—she always had a knack for commanding attention. "Ms., manuscript, and multiple sclerosis." She looked at me.

Ah, of course. And in my mind those three are linked: being an autonomous woman with a right to value and transcribe her own experience, writing the body of the manuscript itself, and having the disease my sister is afflicted with, a multiple sclerotic hardening that leaves dull scar tissue where there was once a filigree of fine nerves.

Gradually, the ms. I wrote in a way replaced her M.S. I thought, at the time, I shouldn't talk to her too much. I might be tempted to write down just what she'd said that morning rather than maintaining the psychic distance to write the best scenes I could. When I'm done writing this, I thought, I'll spend more time with Anita. I was dealing with her life by putting it in a book. It came to seem a bad secret. I kept my pages in a room I went into only when I wrote. I kept the door shut. My monster lived in there.

"I believe my writing is good enough to be punished, I mean *published*," I once said.

In fact, I never wrote the book I planned. I got as far as the foreword, and then turned back to the characters' childhoods, where I remained. I came to love this other book, this unplanned book, and a friend, hearing parts of it, said to my surprise that all the same issues were in there anyway, call them obesity, call them M.S., call them jealousy and stigma and love and guilt.

I didn't trust I could do my sister justice. Writing nonfiction about her disease feels different. As long as I make up nothing, as long as I record as accurately as I can exactly what I witness, then I feel I am respecting Anita. However, I am not comfortable letting my imagination subsume it or distort it, even in the interests of making a more effective scene.

Why? That feels like colluding with God, or with whatever circumstance determined that she would have this disease, in giving it to her. It feels like I am inventing troubles for her. And there's something too sacred, too powerful about the truth to do what feels like playing with the facts, even if it is not really play. I do not want to risk distortion or burlesque. God commanded that Lot and his wife not look back at the cities of Sodom and Gomorrah, which He saw fit to incinerate. Lot strode forward, toward his long life, despite the smell of ash and the shrieks that must have filled the air. But his wife, nameless, rebelled. She looked back at God's destruction, at a face of His she was not supposed to see, and was instantly transformed to salt, her whole being a tear with the liquid burnt off. Some things we cannot see and afterward live unharmed. But if we see these things I think we ought to leave an accurate monument, even if it is just a monument of salt.

I wish I could have written the novel I wanted to. I wish I'd had more respect for my own feelings and vision. I wish I were my younger self come to visit my older. I'd say, "Dive in. Write those hardest scenes first. Of course they'll feel like they're veering out of control. Of course you'll wonder if you'll ever get it right. Do it, and do it over." It is not a sin to write one's truth. We have an obligation to the living, but this includes the inner person living within us, whom we may never know if we do not let her speak.

The friend who shelved her worries so she could write her autobiographical novel told me, "I think it's essential to set yourself outside that sphere of personal consequence for the space of the writing, to free yourself, to forgive yourself, and write what's most true—what's so often both the ugliest and the most beautiful."

Dedalus teaches how to track to the very core of the labyrinth where the half-human beast lives, the rejected, voracious, monstrous child of royal birth, and then how to return to the outside world again without getting lost (all one needs is a length of thread, a spool of words). Inward, inward one travels. Roars echo out. Dead ends and blind passageways, and wild glimpses in sudden mirrors. Dare you go? Have you a right? Dedalus stands for the kind of person who is "dedicated to the morals not of his time but of his art," Joseph Campbell writes. He adds, "He is the hero of the way of thought — singlehearted, courageous, and full of faith that the truth, as he finds it, shall make us free."

At the beginning of its life, Frankenstein's monster was actually a gentle, loving creature. It was the doctor's constant rejection that drove it savage with loneliness. Our monsters may turn to blessings if we regard them with kindness. They may have been blessings from the start, made goblins in the shadowy hallways of our minds. "To deny one's own experiences is to put a lie into the lips of one's own life. It is no less than a denial of the Soul," Oscar Wilde writes. How fine it would be to fully claim our eyes and ears and mouths, to say, "This is what I see. This is what I hear. And this is how I say it. Listen: I say it like this."

DONALD M. MURRAY

LETTER TO A YOUNG ARTICLE WRITER

THE WRITER

Your pieces are filled with interesting, specific information; they have a clear focus; they are well written; but they are not likely to be published without revision.

What they lack is what professionals call an edge. The idea does not contain the tension that attracts and holds a reader. Note the first paragraph of my letter. It contains a surprise, an apparent contradiction, a conflict, something unexpected that engages the reader in a conversation. "What does he mean? The articles are written well, with focused information, and they are *not* publishable?" the reader asks, and the writer responds.

Your articles are pleasant and predictable. They do not have an urgency, a significance, an unexpectedness, a tension that will draw in a reader who is not already fascinated by your subject.

Editors find it difficult to describe what is missing in such good writing—and so do I. The problem is not with what is on the paper but what is not. Editors are looking for what they have not seen and cannot command. If editors know what they want, they can order it from professionals on their staff or from familiar freelancers like me. Doris Lessing said, "You have to remember that nobody ever wants a new writer. You have to create your own demand."

The demand is created when a writer expresses an individual, authoritative point of view toward our familiar world in a voice that is appropriate to the topic and the writer's attitude toward it. The voice communicates authority and concern.

Your ideas do not have an essential tension. Some of my day-book lines that have led to writing include:

"I cheered when we dropped the atomic bomb." [I was in the paratroops and scheduled to jump into Tokyo.]

"I'm lucky I had a sickly childhood." [It forced me to exercise my imagination.]

"I'm glad I have an old wife." [We have a shared history.]

"It was good there was no Little League when I was a kid." [We played sandlot ball and were not over-organized by competitive parents.]

My habit is to seek the tensions within my life and the lives of those around me. I inventory what sparks a strong emotional reaction: irony, anger, despair, humor, pain, pleasure, contentment, fear.

I read the mental and daybook or journal notes I make as I lead my life, asking such questions as:

- What surprises me?

- Where's the tension?

- What should be and what is?

- Where's the conflict?

- Where will these ideas, issues, people collide?

- What's the problem?

- What's different from what I expected?

- What are the implications—for me, for my readers?

- What are the connections?

- What contradicts?

Margaret Atwood says, "Good writing takes place at intersections, at what you might call knots, at places where the society is snarled or knotted up." Mary Lee Settle says, "I start my work by asking a question and then try . . . to answer it."

As I question myself, I hear fragments of language. These are rarely sentences, although they may be. Usually they are just phrases, words in collision, or words that connect in unexpected ways. Recently I wrote a column about my grandson learning to walk. The line came from his father, who said Joshua had "to learn to fall to learn to walk." That was an idea; it contained a truth expressed in a line that had a surprising tension.

I record such lines and scratch when they itch. A lead—the opening sentences or paragraphs—can hold an article in place so I can explore it in a draft written days or weeks later. For example, the other day I was doing errands with my wife when I had the following experience, and I immediately wrote (in my head), "have to get glasses tightened." When I got home, I turned the line into a lead:

> We are driving to Dover, New Hampshire, to shop when Minnie May says, "I have to get my sunglasses tightened."
> I pull up to Whitehouse Opticians and Minnie Mae asks, "Why are we stopping here?"
> "To get your sunglasses tightened."
> "They are home on my desk."
> [She's just talking. I hear a problem to be solved.]

I have an idea, but that's not enough. In John Jerome's wonderful book on nonfiction writing, *The Writing Trade: A Year in the Life* (Viking, 1992), which should be on your desk, he quotes a colleague as saying that a 600-word essay needs about an idea and a half. That articulated an important truth about all articles for me.

My grandson's learning to fall so he could learn to walk was a good idea, but it was not enough. In writing the article I connected his need to learn to fall with writers, artists, scientists, and entrepreneurs, who need to experience instructive failure to succeed. Then I had an essay.

The ancedote demonstrating the difficulty I (who always want to solve a problem) have communicating with my female companion, who is just commenting on life, is an interesting and amusing idea. It articulates a tension most male and female readers have experienced. But it is not yet publishable.

I will write it when I come up with the essential extra half of an idea or, more likely, when I start drafting the piece and discover the extra half during the writing.

Your articles stop short of that significant half of an idea, that moment of discovery of a significant extra meaning that you and your reader share in the writing and reading of the essay.

To find that extra meaning I have to write with velocity so that I am thinking on paper, saying what I do not expect to say. Of course *you* will consider and reconsider, write and rewrite this discovery draft, but for *me*, it is essential to discover what I have to say by saying it. If I know just what I am going to say when I first start to write an article, the draft is flat, uninteresting. When I discover meaning during the writing, as I have in writing this letter to you, I may have something to share with readers that editors will want to publish.

Good luck. Draw strength from the fact that you can gather specific, revealing information; that you can focus it; that you can write a clear running sentence and a paragraph that develops and communicates a thought or feeling, and then go on to find the edge, the tension, that will make editors accept your articles and invite you to write more.

NANCY MAIRS

THE LITERATURE OF PERSONAL DISASTER

VOICE LESSONS: ON BECOMING A (WOMAN) WRITER

A few days before Christmas 1990, hunched on the edge of a folding cot with my laptop computer on a little table drawn up to my knees, I wrote compulsively, hour after hour, as though capturing my world in detail could defer its end. After every few words, I glanced across the top of the screen at my husband, slit and stitched up and webbed in plastic tubing, so wasted and waxy that I had to keep reminding myself: *This is George. You know him. You have loved him for almost thirty years.* "I suppose there are millions of us this very moment in just the same pain," I tapped on the keys. "Why do I feel so *singular*?"

Yes, millions keeping bedside vigils, whispering as I whispered over and over, *Come back! Don't leave me! I need you!*, each of us trapped in this profound and irrational solitude, as though walls of black glass had dropped on every side, shutting out the light, deadening all sound but the loved one's morphine-drugged breathing: I was not, in truth, alone. Was it that intuition which had driven me before, and would goad me again, to write intimately about illness, disability and death? And does the same suspicion provoke others to tell their stories — so much like mine, so absolutely their own? Are we all groping for one another through our separate darks?

Because my books have dealt candidly with my own multiple sclerosis, suicidal depression, and agoraphobia, as well as my husband's melanoma, I am frequently asked to review or endorse works that belong to a distinct though largely unrecognized sub-genre I've come to call, only half-facetiously, the Literature of Personal Disaster. Knowing from painful experience what can happen when one's work falls to a reviewer so unempathic that he wishes not only that one had written some other book but also that one had lived some other life, I'm willing enough to read, on their own terms, first-hand accounts of AIDS (Elizabeth Cox's *Thanksgiving: An AIDS Journal*), freak accidents (Andre Dubus's *Broken Vessels*) and illnesses (Molly Haskell's *Love and Other Infectious Diseases*), manic depression (Kate Millett's *The Loony-Bin Trip*) childbirth gone awry (Anne Finger's *Past-Due*), cancer (Susan Kenney's *In Another Country* and *Sailing*), polio (Leonard Kriegel's *Falling Into Life*), deafness (Carole Glickfeld's *Useful Gifts*), stroke (May Sarton's *After the Stroke*), widowhood (Rebecca Rice's *A Time To Mourn*), to name only a few. These are serious works of fiction and nonfiction, not the print equivalents of the sensational sagas touted by "Geraldo" or "A Current Affair," and they warrant my attention, if not always my affection.

I consider reviewing a professional obligation, and ordinarily I take the books assigned to me rather than select them myself. Thus, I did not choose to be the kind of connoisseur of catastrophe I have gradually become. But what of other readers, the ones a publisher's marketing staff must have in mind when they give an editor the nod for a journal delineating a mother's slow wasting from pancreatic cancer (Le Anne Schreiber's *Midstream*) or the remembrance of a beloved husband, newly dead (Madeleine L'Engle's *Two-Part Invention*)? If, as I have read, something like a thousand new titles are published each week, what do the bookmongers believe will draw readers to these two? Sorrow? Curiosity? What are they supposed to find there? Solace? Reassurance? Sheer relief that, however wretched their own lives may seem, others are worse?

In short: Why do I, and others like me, write this stuff? Why does anybody read it? (Or, to put the matter more cynically but no doubt more accurately, why does anybody think anybody else is going to pay good money to read it?) And what, if anything, happens when they do?

In *A Nation of Victims*, a book more wrong-hearted than wrong-headed, which could have been written only by a well-educated young Euro-American male who appears in his jacket photo to be in the pink of condition, Charles J. Sykes complains that, U.S. society having "degenerated into a community of insistent sufferers," our "National Anthem has become The Whine." If so, then one might reasonably expect the works I'm writing about, founded as they are in pain and loss, to form an analogous National Literature. But in truth, virtually no writer I've encountered has sounded more aggrieved than Mr. Sykes himself. Sad, yes. Frightened, yes. Furious, yes. But almost never plaintive.

The true victim—the person set apart from ordinary human intercourse by temporary or permanent misfortune—has little enough time and evenless energy for sniveling. Illness and death, whether one's own or a beloved's, take *work*, and I'm not using the word metaphorically. There are hands to be held and basins to be emptied and upper lips to be kept stiff. One has to husband one's resources. Self-pity simply doesn't provide an adequate motive for expending precious effort to write about the ordeal. But the work, tough as it is, feels singularly instructive, as though one were taking up a severe and rather odd new discipline, spelunking, perhaps, something that draws one through the stink of bat guano toward an unfathomable abyss. It pricks all one's senses.

The impulse, at least for someone of a writerly persuasion, is not to bemoan this condition but to remark it in detail. Initially, one's motives for translating happenstance into acts of language may be quite private. Catastrophe tends to be composed not of a monolithic event but of a welter of little incidents, many of which bear no apparent relationship to one another, and language, in ordering these into recognizable patterns, counteracts disorientation and disintegration. This process of making sense of a flood of random data also produces the impression—generally quite groundless—of control, which may save one's sanity even though it can't save one's own or anyone else's life.

These therapeutic results provide ample reason for keeping a personal journal, but they don't account for the penchant of some writers (and most of the words I have in mind were written by people who would have been writing *something* anyway) for transforming intimate experience into public artifact. Some may share my aesthetic drive: to transmute dross — my own hastening physical deterioration, my husband's wretched, retching progress through chemotherapy — into lapidary reality. And some may find, as I have done, that they thereby write their way into better behavior than they believed themselves capable of. I am forever publishing brave statements that I must then make good on if I am to be a woman of my word.

I can't always do so, of course, but sometimes I can. And since I possess no extraordinary existential gifts, I assume that you can, too. You will need to, I know. All of us who write of calamity know this before all else: there is nothing exceptional about our lives, however these may differ in their particulars. What we can offer you, when the time comes, is companionship in a common venture. It's not a lot, I know, but it may come in handy. The narrator of personal disaster, I think, wants not to whine, not to boast, but to comfort. As one of the sufferers interviewed in Cheri Register's *Living With Chronic Illness* points out, it is possible to be *both* sick *and* happy. This good news, once discovered, demands to be shared.

This underlying drive to console may account for the fact that more women than men seem attracted to the genre and that the works of women tend to be more intimate and immediate than those of men. This gender difference is not essential but circumstantial: women have traditionally been accorded social permission both to suffer and to mitigate suffering, especially messy suffering, the kind involving fevers, excreta, compresses, and nursery puddings. Men, by contrast, have been supposed to pretend that nothing hurts or frightens them, not the bully's rabbit punches on the playground, not the black tumor gnawing at the entrails, *nothing*, and to sneer at pain and terror in others. Choosing to speak publicly about affliction is risky for both, but for different reasons: for the woman, because the behavior (public utterance) is culturally impermissible; for the man, because the condition (physical or mental weakness) is proscribed. Clearly, the woman who undertakes to publish a book about her miseries, or about anything else, has already decided to transgress, at whatever cost, the taboo on female speech; thus, she has resolved the crucial issue before beginning her project. But a man, who is expected to speak publicly but not to expose his infirmities, may have to struggle with this conflict of (self)interest in the writing itself.

The approved resolution to his problem is to distance the authorial subject from the suffering subject. The author—highly intelligent, perceptive, above all in control—may then scrutinize and explain and interpret pain without ever appearing to fall victim to it. This use of intellect to divorce self from experience may account for the peculiar deadness of a book on madness like William Styron's *Darkness Visible* when contrasted with the third, "depressed" section of *The Loony-Bin Trip*, which forces the reader to pace Kate Millett's narrow, grimy kitchen along with her as she subsists on soda crackers and coffee, unable to write, unable to speak, her attention contracted to a single point: "Oneself. In danger."

That intellectualization is not a strictly gender-bound coping strategy is made clear by Susan Sontag's brilliant but icy *Illness as Metaphor*, which bears no trace of the author's personal encounter with cancer. I don't condemn nonpersonal analysis; on the contrary, I for one need *Illness as Metaphor* to be exactly as it is. But the drawback to an approach like Styron's—openly self-referential yet without intimacy—is that it also distances the reader from an experience she or he may have no other means for understanding. I've *been* mad in just the way Styron has, and even I couldn't figure out from his book what such a state feels like.

Which happens to be fine with me, since I already know. (Not that great, no matter what poets of disaster like Sylvia Plath and Anne Sexton suggest.) But what of the woman who wrote to me after her lover had shot herself to death? She didn't need a description of depression (she was a psychiatrist) but a means of fathoming suicidal despair. She needed to enter and endure it with me. Those writers who seek to console and hearten must make themselves and their anguish wholly transparent, revealing not illness as metaphor but illness as illness, in order to persuade the skeptical reader, through the very writing, that survival (at least till the last page) is possible.

With the exception of the strictly private journal, which lies outside any literary discussion unless its author later decides to change its status, the sense of isolation I mentioned earlier figures powerfully in the writer's impulse to record calamitous events intending to make them public. Publication of any sort is an intrinsically social act, "I" having no reason to speak aloud unless I posit "you" there listening; but your presence is especially vital if I am seeking not to disclose the economic benefits of fish farming in Zaïre, or to recount the imaginary tribulations of an adulterous doctor's wife in nineteenth-century France, but to reconnect my self—now so utterly transformed by events unlike any I've experienced before as to seem a stranger even to myself—to the human community.

The "you" required by such an "I" must be unusually vivid and available, I know as a writer. That is, in writing I construct an ideal reader possessing these characteristics. But I don't expect real readers to share them. Real readers, in fact, puzzle me a bit, the way women puzzled Freud, and I'm terrifically grateful to the ones who write and tell me what they want, which tends to be advice (sometimes), sympathy (often), and (every now and then) the chance to give me pieces of their minds, some of these more palatable than others. Many want simply to thank me for putting their feelings into words. These voices, lending materiality to my readerly ideal, transform monologue into intercourse.

When I take up the role of reader myself, I sense a discrepancy between my own readers, both imagined and actual, who are generally smart, sensitive, and sympathetic, and those some publishers have in mind for their releases. (Or do they have readers, as distinct from consumers, in mind at all?) I don't read the most disastrous disaster narratives, I'm sure, since these never make it as far as the reviewer's desk. Only once have I had to tell a publisher that not only would I not endorse the book he sent me, if I were he I wouldn't even publish it. (He did, and went belly up not long afterward, which gave me less satisfaction than I would have anticipated.) I read nothing written in pop-psyche-speak, on principle, and I lack the background to comment on books, good or bad, dealing with sexual or substance abuse. All the same, too much of what I do read is poorly conceived, clumsily written, and carelessly edited.

Although bad books are published in every genre, I know, I mind these more, perhaps because I feel a certain defensiveness about personal disaster as an authentic literary subject. As people with disabilities who were once shuttered by shame and superstition move out into productive roles in society, and as society is enriched by their participation, we will all benefit from the increase in awareness and information their works provide; and surely we can all use the solace derived from knowing that the grief and fury we feel when "bitten by bad nature," as Sylvia Plath puts it, has been endured by at least one other person. We must take care, however, not to condescend subtly to such authors by lowering the literary standards to which we hold them out of a cynical or sentimental misreading of readers' needs and expectations.

What, if not misplaced pity, prompted an editor to accept for publication a manuscript in the first chapter of which a psychiatrist likens the challenge of psychoanalyzing the raving paranoiac who has just showed up in his tastefully accoutred Central Park office to "trying to make par on a long and winding hole where you cannot see the green as you tee off"? The entire book turns out to be just as shallow as its founding metaphor would suggest. Did the editor consider writers about madness too inept to produce literature of quality? Did he believe that only voyeuristic or prurient readers would be drawn to a book on such a topic, and that they merited whatever they got? Less cynically, did he regard schizophrenia as so urgent a subject that the usual standards ought to be waived in order to broadcast as much information as possible?

Although in some instances (I wonder whether AIDS might be a contemporary case), such a documentary function might justify publication, it cannot by itself make books in this genre work as literature. It's not enough to feel bad nature's bite: to find yourself, having stopped to help two stranded motorists, catapulted by a speeding car into the night, from which you wake to a new life without the use of your legs; to flounder about, baffled and bitter, for some way to prepare your young children for their father's death; to drag yourself, in an ill and aging body, from bed to desk and back again until you weep and wish for death. These are central situations in some of the best work being done in this genre, but by themselves they're merely horrific, not redemptive. Misery, no matter how mysterious and poignant, is not enough to make a book, and if an editor and the marketing strategists who drive editorial decisions think it is, somebody (or preferably a lot of somebodies) has to tell them otherwise.

The trick, with this as with any genre, is to satisfy its requirements while escaping its confines. The writing about personal disaster which functions as literature tends not to be "about" disaster at all. That is, whatever adversity provides the grounds for the project must be embedded in a context both enigmatic and elaborate: the insistent everyday world. For this reason, perhaps, writers already experienced in other genres are apt to accomplish most in this one. The works of the writers I have in mind transcend their separate ordeals to speak generally, and generously, of the human condition.

Andre Dubus, a critically acclaimed writer of short fiction, was indeed struck by a car and crippled permanently in 1986. But *Broken Vessels* is extraordinary not because it depicts physical and emotional trauma but because it demonstrates tacitly, by collecting essays written between 1977 and 1990, the spiritual maturation that suffering can force: "After the dead are buried, and the maimed have left the hospitals and started their new lives, after the physical pain of grief has become, with time, a permanent wound in the soul, a sorrow that will last as long as the body does, after the horrors become nightmares and sudden daylight memories, then comes the transcendent and common bond of human suffering, and with that comes forgiveness, and with forgiveness comes love. . . ." The life that leads one to this point can no longer be termed in any sense disastrous.

Susan Kenney, who has chosen to treat the issues raised by her husband's cancer in fictional form, delineates a similar progress toward sympathetic wisdom as her central characters, Sara and Phil, move ambivalently and ambiguously toward Phil's death. One of the great virtues of both *In Another Country* and *Sailing* lies in Kenney's eye and ear for the comic in even quite grisly situations, as when Phil, in the throes of chemotherapy's nausea, performs spectacularly in front of a traffic cop, thereby sparing Sara a speeding ticket. The memory of this scene buoyed me through many a gastric eruption during George's chemotherapy. The truth is that those of us in calamitous circumstances laugh a good deal, not just because Norman Cousins has told us to, though his was excellent advice, but because funny things go on happening to people no matter what. Kenney's capacity for capturing life's clutter—the way cancer has to fit in among children's tantrums and Christmas shopping and the pressures of work and the death of the old dog—shows suffering in its proper scale, not inconsequential, by any means, but insurmountable either.

Like Dubus and Kenney, May Sarton captures and celebrates the commonplace, in her poems and novels but especially in her journals, of which *Endgame* is the most recent. Over the years, she has drawn her audience into her world—the cats, the lilacs and daylilies and tree peonies, the bottles of Vouvray and champagne, and always the dogged work of a prolific writer—so meticulously that when I was given the chance to call on her last summer, I stepped into a landscape already familiar, salt meadow joining the yellow house with the sweep of the sea. There I met at last the woman who had been teaching me what to love about solitude, about company, for years. She gave me chilled wine and *gaufrettes* and one white rose from her garden.

As Sarton's health has failed, wearing her to translucency, infirmity has surfaced, gradually and naturally, as a major theme in her recent work. In permitting it to emerge instead of painting it over, she communicates a harsh lesson: aging is the one disaster that, if we escape all others, will claim us in the end. As luck and the actuarial tables would have it, most of "us" will be women, many of whom, having endured the grievous loss of a life partner, will suffer both the lack of "the tangible 'we' when two people live together in amity" and loneliness "in essence for the *self*," the former resilient and responsive self, who now creeps crablike across the ice to the car for yet another trip to the doctor who will never again make her well. Eventually, each will say, "I want to die, there's no doubt about that. When you have as much pain as I have and there's no way out you *do* want to die, if you're as old as I am. . . . There is that hope that someday, while you're asleep, the old heart will stop beating."

Yet, in spite of her admission that now "everything hurts," Sarton casts aside "fantasies of suicide as a way out of the constant chronic pain. . . . I feel one must have one's death, one must not make one's own death. One must let death come when the time has come." In the meantime, she writes, not so much about being old and ill as about what matters moment by moment: not a "really appallingly frail and old-looking woman" but the person within, "seeing an awful lot, being aware of an awful lot"—a friend's thick, savory soup, and Pierrot the Himalayan, who looks "like a Roman emperor in cat form," and the house filled with dewy pale pink roses, purple anemones, white and lavender tulips, blue asters. . . . These are books about going on. All the way. To our common destination.

To which none of us wants to go ignorant and alone. Hence, into the dark, we write.

MARGOT LIVESEY

HOW TO TELL A TRUE STORY

AWP CHRONICLE

Nine years ago my step-mother, Janey, died in a small Scottish town. I was teaching summer school at a university near Boston, and her death was, from my perspective, sudden. One morning on my way to class, I found a letter in the mail-box from an aunt; I read it on the bus. My aunt wrote that Janey had had a fall and was in the hospital but not to worry she was making good progress. I don't remember what I taught that day, but I do recall my anger. Her accident, I thought, would mean new problems, new difficulties, for me. I was still angry when the chairman came into my office with a message that Janey was very ill. I hurried home immediately and made arrangements to fly to Glasgow. Then I phoned the hospital, Perth Infirmary, only to discover she was already dead. A week later a birthday card arrived from Janey. A nurse had written the address and a joke about my step-mother's many gentlemen visitors. Janey herself had signed the card, shakily, "love M."

I did not go to her funeral. I knew I would have to return later to deal with her possessions and I was too poor to make two transatlantic trips and too young to understand the complex reasons for which one might attend a funeral where no other mourner would be offended by one's absence. Instead I decided to write a story about her. The question was how?

She was almost fifty when she married my father and I knew only snatches about that large part of her life which had already occurred. I wanted to honor her memory, to be faithful to the facts, as I understood them, including our deep estrangement, and yet to do merely that would have resulted in a skinny, parsimonious, undignified story. I needed imagination as well as memory.

Over the course of a difficult autumn I wrote the story, "Learning By Heart." It was a long story, a hundred pages, with two braided narratives. One strand of the narrative was what I remembered of my childhood and adolescence with my stepmother and I wrote the material as if I were writing an essay. Although I was presenting it as a story I wanted readers to think, oh yes, this really did happen. The other strand was my imagining of Janey's life. The life I did not know and had no means to discover, I dreamed up on the page. And in a number of ways I signaled to the reader that this part of the narrative had a different ontological status, was true in a different way. I wrote it as fiction.

I am not sure how well "Learning By Heart" succeeds but since then, in and out of the classroom, I have pondered how the intuitive choices I made in writing that story might be refined. I began to notice that I often gave my students conflicting advice. A student would bring me a story about a family with three children. Sometimes I would say why do you need Edwina, Margaret, and Theo? It just confuses your reader. Why don't you collapse Edwina and Margaret into a single character and just have two children? Sometimes, however, I found myself saying the opposite. Why only have three children? I would ask. Why not have five? Or go for broke — have seven?

In the first case I was advising the student along the traditional lines of story writing. Be expedient. As Sydney Cox says in his opinionated book *Indirections*, every sentence, every detail should reveal character, deepen the theme, and advance the plot. The pleasure of this kind of narrative is not that we think we are reading about the real world but rather that the wings of symmetry are unfolding around us; briefly we are on a planet where human behavior makes sense. I call this fiction.

In the second case I was clearly suggesting an alternative strategy. The authority of the story was coming, in part, from the degree to which it made the reader feel that the events described really had occurred. And the way to strengthen the story was to increase this effect. Rather than expediency, I urged the student to make the story messier, more confusing, in other words more life-like. I call this anti-fiction.

Throughout this century it seems to me an increasing number of authors have been choosing to have five children rather than two. We can find story after story, novel after novel, where the boundaries between author and character, real and imagined, are blurred and our experience is closer to reading autobiography, or history. I do not mean to suggest that there are simply two, exclusive choices. Rather I see a continuum, stretching from tales beginning "Once upon a time . . ." where we are blithely expected to believe that a wolf can pass for a grandmother, to the most explicit anti-fiction, works whose authors blatantly encourage what Sartre might have termed a hemorrhaging between fiction and reality. In Joan Didion's *Democracy* and Tim O'Brien's *The Things They Carried* characters share the names and occupations of their creators.

Once I got a glimpse of the continuum I wondered what lay behind these alternatives and how the signals were given to the reader. The first question invites a comet's tail of speculations. My suspicion is that most authors make these choices unconsciously, as I did, because of their prior relationship with the material. But at a deeper level, further into the astral debris, lurks the demon of how to give our work authority. By the end of her life my step-mother had very few visitors. What right had I to ask my readers to be amongst them? To endure the wallpaper and the antimacassars and, worst of all, my step-mother's boring, tyrannical conversation.

In a recent fit of homesickness I reread *Dr. Jekyll and Mr. Hyde*, a novel I think of as essentially Scottish that happens to be set in London. As usual I was consoled by the darkness and fog but this time I was also struck by Stevenson's use of documents: letters and Dr. Jekyll's confession. Looking at other nineteenth century novels — *Wuthering Heights, Dracula, The Woman in White* — I discovered a startling number of inter-locking narrators, diaries found in locked boxes, death-bed confessions and, of course, letters. These authors knew that their incredible tales needed authenticating and they approached their readers like a prosecutor a jury, bombarding us with testimonials from expert witnesses.

In this century such devices have fallen out of fashion but not because we have become more credulous as readers. If anything, our credulity has declined and we are liable to read a letter in fiction as yet more fiction. There are gorgeous counter-examples. Part of the brilliance of Nathanael West's *Miss Lonely-hearts* is the inclusion of letters from Miss Lonelyhearts' constit-uents that are absolutely integral to the plot and to the anguished voice of the novel. More recently A.S. Byatt paid homage to the nineteenth century in her novel *Possession* by including fabri-cated poems. The novel captivated many readers but most I sus-pect soon realized that they could follow the plot without reading the poem and turned those pages with increasing speed. Not only have we grown wary of devices but we have decided to privilege memory over imagination, or so it seems to me. In the current climate a novel set in Vietnam, written by someone who had not been there, would be unlikely to meet with the rapturous reception of *The Red Badge of Courage*. Certain experiences — war, other races, some illnesses, perhaps other sexual orientations — are no longer appropriate territory for the imagination. We want the author to be writing out of memory. Even a kind of imper-sonal memory — the American born, Jewish author writing about the Holocaust — is preferable to none. The long tradition of the amateur writer is under siege. Authors, along with other people, are now expected to have credentials.

We are even reluctant to permit an author to write fully about a character of the opposite sex, as witness our overwhelming assumption that first person narrators are the same gender as their authors. In "Learning By Heart" I did not bother for many pages to identify the narrator as a young woman, a version of myself; I knew the reader would think that anyway. These as-sumptions, which can do so much for our work when we follow them, become problematic if we want to contradict them, espe-cially I think for women writing about men. A dozen great fic-tional heroines — Pamela, Moll Flanders, Molly Bloom, Emma Bovary, Anna Karenina — sidle out of my bookcase, swishing their skirts courtesy of their male authors but not a single man, suited by a woman's pen, steps forward to keep them company. Perhaps writing about men is something that most women are not interested in, but one would like to feel sure that it is a genuine choice, rather than a constraint.

Optimistically I like to think that this narrowing of authorial authority has as one of its main origins the widening of the canon, and the general recognition that minorities are willing and able to speak for themselves. But I also wonder if it might not be linked to the surge of anti-fiction. Authors have been encouraging readers to map fiction onto the real world, and even when we want to, we may have trouble now in reversing that trend. Perhaps Lewis Carroll's "Sylvie and Bruno Concluded" might serve as a cautionary tale. In this story Carroll describes Sylvie and Bruno's attempts to find an accurate map. Eventually the two children end up with a one to one map and wreak havoc amongst the local farmers by blocking out the sun.

Putting aside these vexed matters of authority and autobiography I want to explore in a little more detail what makes readers think, just from reading, that some stories really happened and in others that the question is irrelevant? As with the job interview, first impressions are vital, so a good place to look is in the openings of a few familiar works.

Here is Joyce embarking on his great voyage.

> Stately, plump Buck Mulligan came from the stairhead, bearing a bowl of lather on which a mirror and a razor lay crossed. A yellow dressing-gown, ungirdled, was sustained gently behind him on the mild morning air. He held the bowl aloft and intoned:
> Introibo ad altare Dei.
> Halted, he peered down the dark winding stairs and called out coarsely:
> Come up, Kinch! Come up, you fearful jesuit!

There is nothing in these events that renders them immediately fictional. In fact the quotidian subject matter could easily find a place in an essay but Joyce gives us unmistakable signals that we are on the planet of fiction. There is no visible narrator.

The act of writing is concealed. We are made to believe that the words sprang up on the page without effort. Characters are shown to us through action and dialogue. There is no initial attempt at explanation. There is considerable specificity of detail and a kind of heightened density to the style. From our earliest listening and reading we have learned to understand these as the hallmarks of fiction. We are not, I think, allowed for a moment to take this as biography or history.

Here on the other hand is Proust.

> For a long time I used to go to bed early. Sometimes, when I had put out my candle, my eyes would close so quickly that I had not even time to say "I am going to sleep." And half an hour later the thought that it was time to go to sleep would awaken me; I would try to put away the book which, I imagined, was still in my hands, and to blow out the light; I had been thinking all the time, while I was asleep, of what I had just been reading, but my thoughts had run into a channel of their own, until I myself seemed actually to have become the subject of my book: a church, a quartet, the rivalry between Francois I and Charles V.

The paragraph continues to explore this confusion between waking and sleeping, book and self. In his dream-like state the narrator ponders the act of writing: "the subject of my book would separate itself from me, leaving me free to choose whether I would form part of it or no." There is an absence of dialogue and a lack of immediacy; right away we are being told that events are remembered. Most note-worthy of all, we are in the presence of a narrator who is not immediately distinguished from the author. Crucial to *Remembrance of Things Past* is the narrator's situation as an only child and such is the autobiographical force of the writing, that I think almost all readers are amazed to discover that Proust had a brother. Surely we can be forgiven our confusion when Proust not merely tolerates but encourages it. The narrator of this novel is not named for many hundreds of pages, but when at last he is, his name is Marcel.

Over and above all this the basic difference between *Ulysses* and *Remembrance of Things Past* is between the third person and the first. The third person is the "once upon a time" voice that signals we are being told a story. In "Learning By Heart" I was being absolutely conventional when I put the parts about Janey's life that I was largely inventing in the third person and the part that I had actually experienced in the first person. But the way in which I used the first person would not have been possible without the example of Proust. There were, after all, plenty of first person novels prior to *Remembrance* but reading, for example, *Tristram Shandy*, *The Red and the Black*, *Jane Eyre*, we have, I think, no impulse to confuse author and narrator. For one thing, these authors carefully separate themselves from the narrator. Look at the opening paragraph of *Great Expectations*.

> My father's family name being Pirrip, and my Christian name Philip, my infant tongue could make of both names nothing longer or more explicit than Pip. So I called myself Pip, and came to be called Pip.

Could Dickens have mentioned Pip's name a little more often in the first paragraph? Reading on we find in Pip's fanciful description of the tombstones of his relatives the density and the unnatural specificity of fiction and, although events are clearly in the past, neither the act of remembering nor writing is invoked. My first thought was that even a reader who knows nothing of Dickens' early life would suspect that more than the name of the narrator is being fictionalized. But that is the wrong way round. We are being so clearly signaled that this is fiction that the question, "Did these things really happen?" does not occur, anymore than we ask if a wolf in a nightgown would really make a convincing grandmother. This kind of opening was later passionately subverted by Salinger's Holden Caulfield who announces that he is not going to tell us, "where I was born, and what my lousy childhood was like, and . . . all that David Copperfield kind of crap."

In shifting the boundaries between the self and the book, Proust, I would argue, has had a far greater influence than Joyce. A host of fictional memoirs have been published since *Remem-*

brance of Things Past, some of which have sought to extend the continuum of anti-fiction even further. How far this can be done without the reader wondering why this material is being called fiction is a question to ponder. A few years ago the French writer Marguerite Duras, after a long silence, published a short novel, *The Lover*. The novel centers around the relationship between a fifteen-and-a-half year old French girl and her Chinese lover. The American edition had a photograph of the young Duras on the front cover, and it was widely mentioned in reviews that this novel was heavily, if not entirely, autobiographical.

Putting aside these marketing techniques, one of the most obvious things about reading the opening pages of Duras' novel is the way she shuttles back and forth between France and Indochina, between her fifteen year old and her present self. It could I suppose give the effect of muddle or disorganization but in fact it strengthens our sense that the events described have really occurred. Duras is simply remembering and picking out what she wants to tell us. When I went back to "Learning By Heart" I realized I had done the same thing. Janey's story moved steadily forward with the occasional memory embedded in the flow; it was hard enough to make things up without skipping around. But in the part that I was remembering I found it almost impossible to progress chronologically. Describing Janey's marriage to my father, I skipped a quarter of a century to report my reading of the letters she had received at that time. Not one of the twenty odd letters referred to me. The only reason for such an omission could surely be that Janey, in announcing her marriage, had not bothered to mention my existence.

In the nineteenth century Duras would probably have used letters or a sensational secret diary to support her story. Late in the twentieth century, however, she relies upon a heavy hemorrhaging between reality and fiction. No one could attack the plot because she was telling us that these events really happened, but if pressed too closely, she could protest that this was fiction. Several times in *The Lover*, the narrator claims that she has never written about this material before and, now that she is, she plans to tell the whole truth and nothing but the truth. Even fairly soon after publication, however, astute critics were diagnosing a hole in the heart of the novel. And now Duras is agreeing with them. She is advertised as being at work on a new book which will reveal what the scandalous relationship in *The Lover* concealed — namely her incestuous relationship with her brother.

I do not mean to sound as if I am taking Duras to task for mendacity, per se. My concern is not whether the events described in a work of fiction occurred, but rather the techniques by which an author might make a reader believe they did. All authors omit and select. When I discover that Proust has a brother, it does not detract from the beauty and authenticity of his portrayal of an only child. In "Learning By Heart" I described at length my loneliness and isolation. The truth is that for a good part of my childhood we lived near a family with four children who frequently took me in, but I never mention them. I like to think that this omission was not merely a bid for reader sympathy but also a way to clarify the story, to allow Janey and my relationship with her to emerge more clearly. No, my charge against Duras is not the omission but the way in which the omission distorts the material, as, for instance, Dickens' attempt at a happy ending to *Great Expectations* seems to distort all that the novel has been moving towards.

Besides the techniques I've already suggested — vagueness, the invocation of remembering and writing, shuttling, hemorrhaging, the absence of dialogue — I've discovered three more techniques which help to create the illusion of anti-fiction. One, which I do not advocate to my students, is what I'm rather nervously going to call "bad writing." Fiction tends to be well written. A surprising number of characters and narrators reach what, if one stops to think, are quite unrealistic heights of eloquence. It follows then that one way for an author to make their work seem real is by the judicious use of bad writing.

I was a little hard-pressed to find an example of this outside of my own work, but I think you can glimpse what I'm talking about in the opening of Camus's novel *The Stranger*, a novel for which I have great admiration.

Maman died today. Or yesterday maybe, I don't know.
I got a telegram from the home: "Mother deceased. Funeral

tomorrow. Faithfully yours." That doesn't mean anything. Maybe it was yesterday.

The old people's home is at Marengo, about fifty kilometers from Algiers, I'll take the two o'clock bus and get there in the afternoon. That way I can be there for the vigil and come back tomorrow night. I asked my boss for two days off and there was no way he was going to refuse me with an excuse like that.

I am playing the devil's advocate, of course, in suggesting that this is bad writing but what I'm getting at is obvious. The prose is painfully flat, almost to the point of being simplistic. Even though these sentences demonstrate what Carver called "fundamental accuracy of detail," many writers would hesitate to write them. They seem too unadorned, too unliterary, to transport the reader, but at least in *The Stranger* they effectively create a narrator in whose capacity for violence and lack of self-analysis we come to vividly believe. The anti-fiction quality is further strengthened by the uncertainty: "Maman died today. Or yesterday maybe." After all if it's fiction, there is no reason for any vagueness. We can just decide whatever we want.

From these opening sentences Camus leads us forward to the moment of murder. And this is another technique of anti-fiction I want to suggest, although "technique" may not be the correct term. Fiction tends to offer us conventional post-Freudian psychology. Motivation is one of the principal ways in which fiction makes sense. Readers as well as writers are deeply committed to this and even when a writer tries to prevent us from making certain connections, we often insist on doing so anyway. In *Aspects of the Novel* Forster describes plot as the causal relation between events: the king died and then the queen died because of grief. What he did not say was that if the king dies and then a little later the queen dies, the reader will, willy-nilly, link the two events, even if the author tells us firmly that they have nothing to do with each other.

One of the most frightening things about the world, however, is that action and motivation are often not so neatly connected. I would argue that part of what Camus accomplishes is the creation of a much more complex psychological model, a model which partakes not so much of the glibness with which we too often analyze others but of the mystery with which we speak of ourselves. In writing about Janey I felt reluctant to the point of paralysis to attribute motivation to her. She was a giant of my childhood and neither time nor mortality can dwarf her. This was one of the major reasons I wanted my account of our relationship to sound true; I wanted to block both my own and the readers' easy attempts at psychoanalysis.

Lastly as an anti-fictional technique I want to point to what I call the use of history. It is surprising how many stories and novels contain absolutely minimal references to current events, to anything beyond the characters and their relationships. Jane Austen, as has often been remarked, makes no reference to the Battle of Waterloo. This exclusion seems to suggest that both readers and writers yearn in art for a certain kind of transcendence of the every day. It also means that as soon as we start to connect the lives of our characters with the real world, we are taking a step towards making our fiction sound like anti-fiction. For four years of my childhood I attended a girls' school, which I prayed nightly would be closed down or burned to the ground. But as I explain in "Learning By Heart" the major fact in bringing about the closure of the school was not my prayers but the shrinking of British colonies, which led to fewer people working abroad who needed to send their daughters home to be educated.

All these techniques I've been listing, except bad writing, can be found to gorgeous effect in Tim O'Brien's *The Things They Carried*. This book, dedicated to its characters, takes as one of its main themes the connection between fact and fiction. In "How To Tell A True War Story" the narrator says if you ask whether a story is true and the answer matters, you've got your answer.

> For example, we've all heard this one. Four guys go down a trail. A grenade sails out. One guy jumps on it and takes the blast and saves his three buddies.
> Is it true?
> The answer matters.

You'd feel cheated if it never happened. Without the grounding reality, it's just a trite bit of puffery. . . .Yet even if it did happen . . . you know it can't be true, because a true war story does not depend upon that kind of truth. Absolute occurrence is irrelevant. A thing may happen and be a total lie; another thing may not happen and be truer than the truth.

Here I think O'Brien delineates the dilemma of all serious fiction writers. However we approach our work and the world, we are trying to get at that truth that lies beyond absolute occurrence.

Most of the examples I've offered demonstrate the strength of anti-fiction but one of the major hazards of the enterprise can be seen I think in the experiences of a friend who wrote a series of personal essays about Israel. "Very nice," responded an editor, "but who would want to read about you?"

I immediately applied this chilling question to myself. When I stopped to think, it seemed at first glance very odd that on the one hand it would never occur to me to write my autobiography because my life is so pedestrian, and on the other hand I persist in writing stories that are more or less autobiographical. As the editor says, why should anyone be interested in reading about me?

I think the answer lies in the nature of fiction and art in general. Art has the power to transform the world and nowhere is that power more evident than when applied to the unpromising material of the everyday. In the hands of Flaubert the relationship between a poorly educated serving woman and her parrot becomes a subject of resonance and beauty.

In the case of Janey, however, I lacked confidence in my ability to transform and there were too many suitcases of truth that I wanted to smuggle into the story. I would never have got them all onto the planet of fiction. Instead I tried to create the illusion that Janey had lived and died in the way I described. I knew that this illusion could be immensely seductive but if I failed to rise above the anecdotal then the reader would balk and say, but why should I want to read about Janey and you?

Machiavelli urged the Prince in the service of the state to become a great liar. In the service of truth writers, I think, need to follow this advice. I may not be able to control my autobiographical impulses but there is a measure of control to be gained over the way in which I reveal my secrets. Will I send them forth into the world as fiction? Or anti-fiction? Or some mixture of the two? As Proust so simply and elegantly says, "the subject of my book would separate itself from me, leaving me free to choose whether I would form part of it or no. . . ." Writers are always present in their work. The question is how.

ALLAN GURGANUS

(AS TOLD TO NAOMI EPEL)

I DREAMED THE STORY OF A DREAM

WRITER'S DREAMING

In my book *White People*, there's a story called "It Had Wings." The derivation of the story is completely connected to a dream. Some years ago I had a dream in which I was standing at a kitchen sink in a suburban house, like the one I grew up in when I was a little kid, and I saw something fall in the backyard that was the color of a Caucasian. It fell with a kind of smack onto green grass near a picnic table. It seemed to have fallen from about five miles up in the sky, straight down into this little yard. The thing that I remembered when I woke was the sound it made hitting. It was a sound that I registered on the page, when I finally wrote the story, as *thwunk*. I knew that the thing had wings. The phrase "It had wings" was a part of the dream. I saw it sort of emblazoned, like the motto in Latin over the door to a library. I woke up thinking, What an incredibly beautiful set of words! "It had wings." It seemed to me one of the most perfect sentences that I'd ever thought of. And it was sort of presented to me on a tray in the dream.

Years later—there's often a delay in between having a dream and finding a use or place for it—a composer called me up and said, "I'm looking for a story to set to music. Do you know of anything three pages long that I could use?" I couldn't think of anything immediately. But I used this occasion to write the story "It Had Wings." In this story, an old lady, retired from selling formal wear at Wanamakers for seventy years, is standing at her kitchen sink and sees an angel fall in her backyard. The first thing you see is the angel falling, and then the old lady attempting to minister to this wounded angel and helping him fly away. It was a perfect image in some ways for dreams because part of the gorgeousness of dreams is that nobody knows you actually had them except by your own witness and testimonial. So that if you tell me a gorgeous image, I don't know if you're just sitting here making it up or if you actually dreamed it at night. But in some ways it doesn't really matter because it's all a dream.

What I had to do, and what I always have to do, is find the character to whom this happened. Character is the center of fiction for me. To have that event chronicled in the third person in an abstract way means nothing. It only means something insofar as it relates to the life and experience and readiness of a single person who's open enough to the fact of an angel in her backyard to take her cup and go out and feed the angel a little milk and ask him questions about heaven. And his answer is, "We're just another army. Don't expect much. We miss it here. Notice things more. We're just another army." And I think that that's true. I think that we're all waiting to be transformed into something else but in fact the luckiest of us are the people who realize that this is it. And that to honor our dreams and to honor our loved ones and to honor our rituals and our lives is precisely what literature is endlessly trying to teach us. That this is the moment. And that we are happy and immortal only insofar as we know and notice that.

Finding a shape for the story was enormously satisfying. I wrote twenty-two pages and then boiled it down to three and a half pages. Partly because of the requirements of the composer but also it was such a joy to have been given this kernel of something and then to develop it and to find its larger meaning. It's one of the stories that speaks to me of the subject of dreams with a special resonance.

I think storytelling is inherently curative. I went recently to an AA meeting with a friend and listened to forty people tell their stories, sometimes in three or four sentences. "Hello, my name is George and I'm an alcoholic. My mother drank. My father drank and then I drank and one day I . . ." Suddenly you're in the middle of a narrative which is inherently curative. In the middle of another person's dream, another person's reality.

There's a strange combination in writing of using images and fragments from actual dreams, but also finding a way to have a governed conscious dream life, which is what writing is. Which is what being an artist is. It's to have access to your own unconscious but also to direct it and to be able to drag in facts and figures that you've found that please you: stories that you overhear as well as stories that you make up. The joy of being a storyteller is precisely that I have two dream lives, at least two: the one that happens the eight hours a night that I close my eyes, and also the one that happens the rest of the time when I open my eyes. That's because I can pull images from that literal dream life and also have this rich kind of alternative sideboard, this kind of sidecar on the motorcycle where you have a measure of control that is all too rare in the world now.

Writing is a kind of free fall that you then go back and edit and shape. I think the best things that I've ever got as a writer come frequently all in a burst. You don't ask too many questions at the outset. You can analyze belatedly and retrospectively but there's a kind of physiological sensation that happens when you are really on the trail of a story. When I'm working well, I wear a moving man's zip-up uniform because I perspire so freely that I sweat my way through the fiction. Finally the body is the ultimate testing ground of what works and what doesn't on the page.

When you think about the English alphabet, twenty-six letters, pictograms, that are asked to bear all the human investigations and all the aspirations and appetites that we have and that have ever existed in human history, it's terribly abstract. It's beyond algebra, so that making that abstraction real, to me, as a very physical person, means to enact it physiologically. One way I do that is to read everything I write out loud many many many times. All the stories in *White People* have been read aloud at least thirty or forty times so that there's a kind of ear music that operates as an editorial principal on the page even when a reader is not moving his or her lips. There's a kind of rhythmic synchronicity which sets up in their biological chemistry, which somehow pulls them rhythmically into the fiction and creates a kind of heartbeat on the page. You only get that, I think, by reading the work aloud endlessly.

There are so many things you can do on the basis of these twenty-six letters. You weep, you laugh, you get turned on, you get hungry. It's pretty basic in some ways. By trusting my body and by making that my active collaborator, Hammerstein to my Rodgers, I have a kind of company in the isolation of working.

We all have our own crazy rituals. I pace. I say lines out loud a lot. I live alone and my neighbors think I have a very active and busy apartment. All the voices are me and mine or us and ours. I don't know which. That for me is maybe the greatest fascination. It's how many voices are packed into this single voice? It's how populated each of us really is. Not only with the people that we might've become if circumstances historically and personally had been different—if daddy had not bought the farm in 1936, if I'd been born black instead of white, or if I'd been born in Africa instead of America—but how many other possibilities are encoded in us narratively?

In my first book, *The Oldest Living Confederate Widow Tells All*, I imagined myself into the body of a slave named Castalia who was abducted from Africa when she was three years old, along with her royal family tribe. There was something that happened when I was writing that chapter, about coming out of the river Niger into the ocean and crossing to the slave auction at Charleston, that was almost like a memory. It was not just a kind of narrative invention that I was cooking up detail by detail, knowing that I got this detail from anthropology and this detail from something I'd overheard. It was almost like a preexisting map. And I knew when I imagined the ship turning a bend in the river what was going to be there next. It was just a question of mapping it. So, I think when you're really cooking, when you're really sweating so freely that you have to wash your moving man's uniform every other day, you know that you're in touch with a kind of waking dream life that frequently is the one that hooks up with the most people, the most readers.

It's mistaken to say that you go into a kind of dream state and come out with a 719-page novel. It's a combination of knowing when to be trusting and when to be suspicious. It's a question of knowing when to let the pages flow and then having the good sense to come back and say, "This is better than that. This has to go." It takes a strange combination of being enormously intellectual and willful and smart and also being as trusting as a baby. There are lots of very smart people and there are lots of very trusting people. But it's very hard to get both of them together in one body. That's why there are so few great artists and so few great books. You either get a sweet trusting book or you get a smart cold book.

It's an odd combination of being ruthless, in the sense that you can't be sentimentally attached to an image just because you have had it. You have to be pure in the service of your characters. And it's precisely that seeming selflessness, that giving up of your own ego and your own willfulness, and your own self-congratulatory "Look at me, aren't I brilliant?" that purifies and lets you become clear and at one with the character that you're seeking to save.

I think that the first impulse in writing is to flood it out, let as much run freely as you possibly can. Then to take a walk or go to the bank or go to the store and come back in a day or six months later. To read it with a cold eye and say "This is good. This is not. That sentence works. This is magical. This is crummy." You have to maintain your critical sensibility and not just assume, because it was an extraordinary dream for you, that it will be a dream for other people. Because people need maps to your dreams.

My dreams often tend to be fairly literal. It's almost like a ticker tape comes across the bottom that says "Order flowers for your mother's birthday tomorrow." "Invest in salt mines." I have pretty hardheaded dreams in some ways. They can be very lavish in terms of stage values and special effects but they tend to be about people in situations, on expeditions or errands. It's very hard to typify a good night's dreaming. I tend to remember a lot of images in the morning. I tend to have at least three or four moments from my dreams and, as everybody understands, you can train yourself to do that. I've found it very valuable and entertaining. I tend not to talk about it a lot to other people because I feel that, until you've found out what a dream means and translated it into action, it tends not to be as magical for other people as it is for you. But I always assume that the dreams mean something and part of my joy is decoding the dream. "What does this mean? Oh, I see, I overheard that in the bus and I made that connection to my anxiety about this." It's not that I think I'm infallible at reading my dreams. Part of the beauty of dreams is that they're eternally mysterious. And that's part of their meaning and power for us. They seem to have a kind of wisdom that we don't have in our waking lives. But they have narrative beginnings, middles and ends the way my stories do.

I believe in Whitman's vision that we're all composed of a thousand voices and that those of us who have chosen to use our imaginations on a daily basis instead of suppressing our imaginations, which is what the culture frequently demands, are very lucky because we are always in company. We are always surrounded by voices that are like and unlike our own and that are our own. And part of the joy of having written for twenty-odd years is that as I'm now sitting here, I seem to be alone but in fact I'm trailing about sixty people. They're people that I've created but also people that I've actually, to be more precise linguistically, *discovered* because they preexisted me. They've always been around and waiting to be heard.

When I'm really doing it right, I know not only what's in my characters' wallets, which is what the creative writing classes tell their students you should know, but I could tell you what the great-grandmother's wallet was like and generationally, class-wise, historically, where the matrix that made this particular person possibly came from. Genetically and in terms of nationality and in terms of aspirations. It's like Stanislavsky's admonition to actors to always know everything about your character so that even when you just scratch your back on stage you're scratching your back in a context.

It takes work. Not necessarily on paper. I don't have dossiers for everybody but one example would be that when I started

Oldest Living Confederate Widow I recognized, on the basis of the first thirty pages, that I was writing in the voice of an ungrammatical woman. She said "ain't" a lot. She was very colloquial in her speech and yet I was confused because I thought she was from an upper-middle or upper-class small-town family. That interests me very much, to have a character who can go anywhere but chooses a particular perspective. I was confused about why she was saying "ain't," so I typed "Why I say ain't" at the top of the page. And that became a chapter which was my explanation to myself. It turns out that Lucy Marston had a working-class farm father and an upper-class socialite debutante mother and opted to speak in the voice of her father because she found her mother pretentious and overweaning. So you wind up explaining things to yourself.

I wanted to create the ideal companion, the best company in the world. Lucy, who had a fifth-grade education and lived to be ninety-nine, is a born survivor, a great storyteller and a person who saves her loved ones by imitating and remembering them. So that creating her meant creating her community. All novels are about communities in time and how time changes communities and what parts of communities are not changed and altered by mortality. They're all about accountability. How much I owe you and how much you owe me and how far I can go in helping you. And where that jumping off point is where, much as I care about you and much as I love you, you're on your own. And I'm on my own. Those kinds of basic transactions that are tribal are really at the center of fiction and at the center of our lives.

I've tried to conceive in Lucy of a single voice that was capable of delivering a choral work, a titanic kind of humanity and majesty. So that a single voice could register all the concussions of history and yet come back with a kind of Pan's pipe song, a kind of ebullient folk music, that pulls her through and gets us through.

What you need to be to create a character is terribly hard-headed and sensible. You say, I will now create a ninety-nine-year-old woman. Where is she? She's in a charity rest home. She doesn't have any money left. She gave it all away. Who does she see in the course of a day? She sees the people who help her.

Who are they? There's a nurse and, because it's a low-paying job, probably a black nurse. And how do we make the black nurse particular? Well, he's gay and he's swishy and he wears a T-shirt that says "Disco Ain't Dead Yet" and he makes quilts for people, and he does massages for old people and he does their hair and he does whatever they will pay him to do to get pleasure in their last days. So that by virtue of a process of elimination and by paying enormous attention to how most people live, you wind up concocting a very particular person out of that situation. And they take on a life of their own. Then your obligation is, having set this set of circumstances in motion, to then take dictation from those precepts, those points of the compass. And to trust your own creations to lead you and to tell you what they are like and what they consider funny and how they would, in fact, connect to her.

One of the joys of Lucy, and living with her for seven years (she's the longest monogamous relationship of my life), is that she overattributes. She's a person who, unlike most us, gives more credit than she probably should. She thinks Jerome, who has a high school degree and is, to the naked eye, a very swishy and temperamental queenly gentleman, is the most talented person she's ever met. He can do quilts, he can lip sync Olivier's soliloquies off records he borrows from the public library. He is utterly adorable and important to her. She lets us see his larger capacities and his possibilities, which have been cut off by his circumstances, by the facts of his race and his life and his time. But through Lucy's eyes we suddenly see him as a heroic figure. And at the same time we understand that he's just this swishy orderly. The joy of living in her eyes for those years was precisely that I found myself mythologizing everybody who came in contact with her. Not just the grand figures but people like Zondra the candystriper, so that by the time you finish a book there is a new additional wing in your own interior mansion. You become a bigger and more comprehensive soul by having followed this identity to its logical conclusion as a storyteller.

My characters have made guest appearances in dreams. Little cameos. The strange thing is that other people, who've read the novel, have written me about visitations in their dreams by characters from the book who wind up doing surprising things. That's one of the incredible things about having published a first novel that sold a million and a half copies. It would seem that a writer is dreaming for other people but this strange transaction happens, which is a classic sort of Jungian archetypal situation, in which the initial dreamer is relieved in a kind of relay and then his readers begin dreaming for him. So that if you really tell a story—and for me that's the holy unity—that becomes the history of your readers, then they begin telling you stories that grow out of your own stories.

Somebody told me that at the Convention of Manager-Directors of Old Age Homes in America the keynote speaker opened by reading my description of Larry, the manager of the old age home where Lucy lives. He's a sweet, fat sort of mama's boy who knows everybody on a first-name basis, knows everybody's stories and tries to make this impoverished cinder block building a home. This was read as a description of the ultimate manager of such a place and as a kind of testament to what these people should be doing for the old people who are dependent on them.

It's an astonishing thing to have created a person alone in your room, which then becomes an exemplar for his whole occupation. It's an enormous privilege. And the paradox is, that instead of making you feel puffed up with pride and ego, it's hugely humbling. It sounds like something you say in interviews but it's actually completely and utterly true that you feel that your relation to your readers is a sort of priestly relation. And you realize that there's a reason that, in the original Catholic Church, priests were not allowed to have sex with any one person. Because if you deny yourself a certain kind of genital contact with a single individual you then give away that spirit, that translated libidinal energy, to the little old humpback lady whom you would never consider touching. And to children and to old people and to everybody. And it's that transaction, of reaching into your own dream life, your own smartness, your own aliveness, your own knowledge of the world and handing it over to other people— the extraordinary way in which they then give it back to you quadrupled — that becomes an incredible metaphor, not just for art, but for life. Because all the real metaphors apply to both dimensions. If you are one of those people who gives everything away, what you get back is so enormous, so rewarding and so strengthening that it gives you the kind of courage and energy that you need to go back and find more stories. And to turn them back over to other people.

I had a dream when I was about eight years old that was one of those dreams that's so real you're sure that it's happening. You can't quite believe that you've imagined it because all the details are in place. They say God is in the details and that's certainly true in this case. I was in my knotty pine bedroom in my maple bed with the bed quilts pulled up over me — the history of the locomotive across my bed quilt — and I heard a sound in a black walnut tree right outside my window. That was strange. It was a kind of shuddering, tinsely, rustling sound. I leaned out of my bed and looked and I saw the tail of an enormous beautiful bird. We're talking about a bird that was probably forty feet long from head to toe. It had a kind of peacock tail and the feathers were as big across as palm bows. It was the most ravishing thing I'd ever seen. It was all the colors. All those rich blues and greens and purples and reds that you see in a peacock, but it was a huge, seemingly mythological bird that had somehow come to rest in our tree outside my room. We lived in a ranch house. It was a long, long house and my room was on the far end. And I had this terrible dilemma. I wanted more than anything else for other people to see the bird. I wanted so much to have an audience because I wanted to be confirmed that it was not a dream. That it was reality. Of course there's an ego connection here. I wanted credit for having found it. I wanted to be the tour guide so I had to make a decision about whether to stay in bed and enjoy it and see it a long long time or whether to run and make a noise and risk having it not be there when I brought the others from the far end of the house. I made the decision in the dream when I was a kid to just sit there and watch it. That, in some ways, I was all the witness that I needed and that I didn't need to enlist other living bodies and witnesses in order to have it real.

That seeing it for myself, which, of course, meant dreaming it and inventing it for myself, was all the reality I needed. And so I got an extra fifteen minutes with this extraordinary creature who was preening itself. Probably on the way to Miami Beach. I don't know. But it was a great seminal dream for me.

I guess the message was that the audience was in me. That I was the jury and that rather than jeopardize the experience by enlisting a kind of outward affirmation of the experience, my responsibility as an artist and a dreamer and the keeper of the tree as a kid was to notice as thoroughly as I could. To drink it all in because I knew that I would never see this magical creature again and that the very act of trying to prove it meant that I lost it. Saving it was being alone with it in the moment and drinking it in forever.

LESSONS OF A LIFETIME

THE WASHINGTON POST BOOK WORLD

As I head toward my 87th birthday, I have the good fortune to serve as assistant to two distinguished professors of creative writing: Fall term I will be in a high-caliber small religious college in Florida, Eckerd in St. Petersburg; spring term at the enormous University of Texas in Austin, which has 48,000 students on campus and 23 highly specialized libraries in which to work.

It is a thrilling and rejuvenating experience to work with young people who range from 17-year-old undergraduates to postgraduates of various ages. But as I read their papers and contemplate their increasingly difficult next steps in the writing profession, I am awed by the memory of how relatively easy it was for a young writer to make his or her way in the 1930s as opposed to how frustrating it is now.

In those days the rule was simple: Place four really good short stories in the popular magazines or three in the library journals, and New York publishers will come knocking on your door, asking you to try a novel. And back then there were almost a dozen monthly and weekly magazines that published three or four short stories in every issue: the *Saturday Evening Post, Colliers, Redbook, Ladies Home Journal, Liberty*, and a journal which I peddled door-to-door when I was a boy, but whose name I cannot now recall.

If a young aspirant had a modicum of skill and a busy typewriter she or he would sooner or later get a foothold in one of the magazines and a leaping start on the ladder upward. After

I sold two short stories to the *Post* in 1946, two book publishers expressed an interest in my future writing and one of the magazines mentioned above offered me a most enticing editorial job. I decided to stick with writing.

How different the publishing scene is today; how infinitely more difficult for the beginning writer. Most of the magazines that nurtured new talent in my day no longer exist, and those that have survived publish little fiction. A recent copy I saw of *The New Yorker* had no fiction at all.

To gain a foothold today requires not only skill but also fortitude, the ability to accept temporary rejection, and in some cases, a liberal amount of sheer brass. What do I tell my young students about this?

First, learn to master the English sentence in all its richness of expression and variation in structure.

Second, acquire an individualized vocabulary on at least three social levels, including modern street lingo.

Third, familiarize yourself with the fine books that have already been published so that you can acquire a sense of where fiction or nonfiction is heading. Because I was classically trained I used to believe that one had to know Chaucer, Dante, Balzac, Dickens, Dostoyevski, George Eliot and Thomas Hardy. I no longer believe that. A young person with a good education can learn the secrets of good writing by reading the best contemporary writers: Albert Camus, Gunter Grass, John Updike, Toni Morrison and Joyce Carol Oates, for example. But a wide historical knowledge of books is still a tremendous asset.

Fourth, use every device in the repertory to get to know people in the publishing business who might be of help later on. Editors, publicists and agents circulate looking for talent and are approachable. Go to where they are likely to be. Introduce yourself, get to know them or, more important, enable them to know you. This leads to my fifth and last suggestion.

Consider applying to one of the writing programs sponsored by a good university. The one at the State University of Iowa has a solid reputation, but I also have high regard for the University of Houston's. The new multidisciplinary Master of Fine Arts program in writing at the University of Texas at Austin has high hopes but no track record as yet. Programs at such universities as Princeton, Columbia, Northwestern, Missouri and Stanford have produced professional writers. One of the virtues of such institutions is that in them the student will meet professionals who might be of help later on, among both the professors and the visiting lecturers.

Here are four examples of what can happen in student-teacher relationships in such places, all taken from my work at the graduate level with young people who have already made a serious commitment to writing. I asked my students to compose an imaginary letter to a real publishing house, asking permission to submit an outline and three sample chapters of either a fiction or nonfiction book.

One student, a gifted and highly sensitive black woman, turned in such a brilliant outline for a book on the experiences of black people in conservative Texas that, when she finished reading her proposal, I said, "You write that book, you'll find a publisher."

Another, a young California writer, had several appealing ideas for her next effort, but in the middle of the term she received assurances that if she hurried over to Bosnia, officials there would help her research an account of how Muslim women were treated by the Serbs in their brutal crusade of ethnic cleansing. When she asked me what she should do, I said, "Catch the next plane to Sarajevo. The other subjects can wait."

An interesting pair were extremely gifted students who could never seem to come to grips with the realities of publishing. They ran the risk of becoming the idle drifters who wander from one graduate school to another. They happened to come to my office at the same time, with nothing done on the assignment.

One I will call Martin, a dreamy-eyed lad from the bilingual society along the Rio Grande, had a foot in both the Mexican and Texas worlds. He went off after our conversation and returned with an exciting draft of a short story illustrating the values of the two societies, their friction points, and their hopes for the future. I was ecstatic: "Martin, you get this written, I know you'll find a publisher. This subject will be on the front burner for the next half century. Make your statement now."

His partner in apathy, whom I will here call Vanessa, was a bright woman from Maine of whom teachers said: "She's got to be better than whatever she's showing us in this class. Let's give her another shot." Well, her second attempt was a short story with a brilliant solution to the writer's constant problem: How does the girl meet the boy? She wrote about a reclusive nerd who haunts a library to eye an extremely shy girl whom he does not know how to approach, unaware that she sits in her isolated carrel just as eager to meet him. I couldn't see that the story was going to accomplish much until the girl secretly scans the books he is reading in an orderly fashion and slips into the pages of his next probable choice the following message: "The Chinese Circus is coming to the fair field on Friday. I have tickets."

It was so perfect, so cleverly contrived and accurately phrased that I said it straight out in class: "Vanessa, for two years you've bewildered me. Endless promise but no execution. But this is the most exciting solution to the boy-meets-girl requirement I've come upon in years. You can be a writer. Now get to it."

We have our failures, too, people who have no skill with words, no vision, no realistic likelihood of ever telling a story well. They are what one of my colleagues describe as "People who want to have written a book." They don't fantasize about the hard work of actually writing it. They're the ones who, in the question-and-answer period, always ask more questions about finding an agent than about the actual process of writing.

At my age I can't afford to waste my time on such dawdlers. I seek the young person trying to master her or his craft, who dares to grapple with new subject matter and who, perchance, may have a burning vision of how to express old truths in new forms.

CAROLYN G. HEILBRUN

WOMEN AND BIOGRAPHY

CULTUREFRONT

When Gloria Steinem began her book on self-esteem, which would eventually be published as *Revolution from Within*, she first produced what she characterized as "250 pages of psychological research, anecdotal examples, and philosophical prose." She found the process rewarding, working alone with her computer and her cat. But a therapist friend who read the 250 pages said, "I don't know how to tell you this—but I think you have a self-esteem problem. You forgot to put yourself in."

The publisher of *Revolution from Within* also urged her to include autobiographical elements, certain that, however successful the book might be without them, it would sell even more if she included her own experiences. Steinem's book is ultimately one-fourth autobiography, and there can be little doubt that without this fourth it would have been far less successful or persuasive.

Can we say the same about *biographies* of feminist women written by feminist women? If Steinem's account of the necessity of self-esteem for women—and, as she is at pains to point out, for men—gains greater authority from its autobiographical elements, does it indicate that a biography of a woman who has come to grips with her disadvantages as a female in a male-dominated world gains authority by including, as many recent works of this sort have, the memoirs or struggles of the biographer?

The answer, I suggest, is NO.

We do need to develop clear ideas about the relationship of a feminist biographer to her subject. By encouraging biographers of women to recount their experiences and ideas, we can perhaps develop some useful practical guidelines.

Why just for biographers of women? Because the male biographer's relation to his male subject has been so long established, and his permission to write biography so long assumed, and because he has so many models to call upon, no specific guidelines need to be developed for biographers of men.

Even eccentric models by male biographers, past and current, flourish. A.J.A. Symon's *The Quest for Corvo*, begun with the personal search for an elusive and mysterious subject, Fr. Rolfe (Baron Corvo), established an admirable form for the combination of a biography and an account of the search entailed in that biography. Currently, Calvin Trillin's *Remembering Denny* recounts not only the story of Trillin's Yale classmate who committed suicide but inevitably, as Trillin skillfully makes it appear, aspects of his own life that reflect off his subject's: Trillin does not so much combine biography and memoir as make his own memories indispensable to his biography. Before Symons, Lytton Strachey had offered a new model of biography, for a time displacing the old-fashioned account of a (supposedly) exemplary life, which has, however, returned in the excruciatingly detailed biographies of Joyce, Yeats, Hemingway, Faulkner, Conrad, and others. If the revelation of all facts about women's lives presented complex questions of taste and morals, it was acceptable in biographies of males, with the possible exception, until recently, of the subject's sexual adventures. The shift in the attitude toward revelations of male sexuality is vividly evident if one compares the Roy Harrod biography of John Maynard Keynes with the recent Robert Skidelsky version.

Male biographers of women have always been in a different category than women biographers: they can avoid the powerful urge to identify directly or personally with their subject. I have mentioned elsewhere that, before the current wave of the women's movement, men were the better biographers of women because they could recognize ambition and self-assertion when they saw them without feeling cultural pressures to explain away such unwomanly characteristics. Michael Holroyd, who is writing the authorized biography of Doris Lessing, may, for example, face new and different problems in writing a famous woman's biography today, but he will not identify with her so closely that the identification itself becomes an issue.

Women biographers have had to invent and refine the skills necessary to their craft. That they have done so largely in the last two decades is undeniable. They have rescued themselves from the misconceived requirement—best represented in Elizabeth Gaskell's biography of Charlotte Brontë—of proving that their subjects, though ambitious, revolutionary, and successful, were *really* women.

One major problem still remains: the relation of the biographer to her subject as it appears in the published biography. Women biographers wrestle with this issue ceaselessly; the easiest solution is for the writer to exclude herself, or appear to exclude herself, from the final account of her subject's life. Judith Thurman's brilliant biography of Isak Dinesen proceeds without any personal comment from the author. Thurman has, elsewhere, recounted her difficulties in writing the biography, primarily the dislike of her subject that she developed in the course of her work; eventually, that distaste dissipated. This is nowhere mentioned in the published biography.

Elizabeth Young-Bruel believes the biographer should be present only as a "pane of glass" through which the facts about the subject can be perceived. Her outstandingly satisfying biographies of Hannah Arendt and Anna Freud provide two examples of this approach. The first was criticized, however, for the omission of Young-Bruel's own long experience with Arendt as her student, and the second for the lack of any information about the author, which made it difficult for the reader to pass judgment on the writer's conclusions: for example her conclusion that Anna Freud and her lifelong companion, Dorothy Burlingham, never had a full sexual relationship. This assumption could have been reached on the basis of many factors, but we were never told what its actual basis was. In such a case, the reader is left in some doubt as to the qualifications of the biographer to make such a judgment. To avoid ambiguity, I have come to believe that it is desirable, even necessary, for women biographers of women to tell the reader—in the introduction, footnotes, endnotes, or perhaps occasionally (very occasionally) parenthetically in the text—where "they are coming from."

A good example of how this may be handled is Deirdre Bair's fine biography of Simone de Beauvoir. In an excellent introduction, Bair explains how she came to write the biography, her experiences with Beauvoir's life and ideas, what it was like to work with Beauvoir, what methods she used, and what emotions she discovered in herself. Bair is thereafter absent from the biography, except in the endnotes. She was convinced that any comments from her during the course of the biography should properly be relegated to the endnotes, which can, and have, been read almost as a variation on her undertaking and as a virtual handbook on the writing of biography.

In the early years of women writing women's biographies, several authors made fascinating attempts to vary the male form of biography. Carol Ascher, for instance, interrupted her biography of Beauvoir (it long preceded Bair's) to include a letter she wrote to Beauvoir expressing Ascher's anger at, among other things, Beauvoir's lifelong devotion to Sartre. She placed the letter in the middle of the published biography, and it helped many of us to accept and examine our complex attitudes to our subjects and to feminism. Even Bair, herself, tells us, to our great benefit, that she had promised to show the final manuscript to Beauvoir—certainly a problematic decision—but had been enabled by Beauvoir's death to avoid the issue.

Through the decades it became increasingly clear that the relationship of the biographer to her female subject was a parlous one, for the obvious reason that feminism itself was risky, that radical assaults upon the assumptions of the patriarchy were frightening, for oneself and one's subject. What also became clear is that the relationship of the female biographer to her mother, a relationship that has not yet been adequately explored or defined (and one that Freud egregiously ignored or misunderstood) has a frightening way of surfacing when a woman writes about her subject's relation to *her* mother.

Bell Gale Chevigny, in her celebrated essay of the early eighties, "Daughters Writing: Toward a Theory of Women's Biography," did much to illuminate the problem. "[F]or feminist biographers, the new engagement with feminist theory, with our subjects, and with ourselves might introduce . . . an inadequately acknowledged vicariousness" projected by the biographer onto her subject. Chevigny explained that it is essential to recognize that "female autonomy cannot be experienced without a sense of abandoning the mother and, by extension, other women and even aspects of the self."

At the same time, it is also essential not to turn women's biographies of women into memoirs of the biographer. To separate the two strands, as Chevigny shows, is far from easy, but is nonetheless imperative. We must work out our relationship to the subject, and our own inner struggles as feminists, but probably we ought not to incorporate these struggles and discoveries into the published biography beyond the introduction and the notes.

Autobiography is a wholly different matter: many perceptive articles have been written on the self as subject and on the problems arising from the fact that the autobiographer's testimony is circumscribed by her own race, class, age, and sexual orientation. Autobiography is, nonetheless, an expanding form for women, and is, like the memoir, the proper medium for personal history and self-discovery. Feminist literary criticism has also learned to make dazzling use of the personal. Having happily abandoned the Olympian tones of male criticism, it has demonstrated that the personal allied with the critical provides more perceptive and wider-ranging literary analysis.

But to return to biography. However essential it may be for the biographer to establish her own voice, perspective, and range of experience for the reader, the self-discoveries revealed to her during the writing of the biography have no place, beyond the introduction, in the finished work. Vivian Gornick, for example, whose *Fierce Attachments* is surely one of the best memoirs of our time, came to recognize that an earlier biographical study had failed because "I was deeply disturbed, and I just let all the disturbance hang out all over the page. . . . One of the failings of that book was the absence of control and proper distance." In short, she had intruded memoir into a biography. Proper distance and control is important to an autobiography as to a biography, but they are the very essence of the latter. The story of the biographer's personal quest belongs elsewhere.

I began with a reference to the biography of Gloria Steinem that I am writing, and I end with something I have learned from writing it. Chevigny has mentioned that, in writing feminist biographies, we often feel the need to rescue our subject from her earlier anti-feminist biographers. Steinem has, God knows, been attacked by anti-feminists, but she has not had her feminism explained away by well-meaning but ill-informed biographers. A living subject has few advantages — the testimony of her contemporaries being the greatest — but, the impulse to rescue her from earlier interpreters who dared not even mention feminism is happily absent.

ANN BEATTIE

WHERE CHARACTERS COME FROM

MISSISSIPPI REVIEW

I'm often asked whether I'm annoyed by being asked the same questions over and over. Quite often the question is asked by someone who has invited me to read and to answer questions afterwards, or by an interviewer hoping to provoke me. The short form of my answer is always, "No," but usually some qualifications are thrown in. There are questions, for example, I am asked by the press or by teachers of creative writing that I've never been asked by anyone in an audience or in a classroom. There are times when questions are so particular to the questioner that I'm at a disadvantage if I can't find out quickly (by subtle questioning) why they asked. There are a few — but only a few — truly boring questions. Even then, my reaction usually has to do with when in the interviewing process they are asked. If the first question is, "Where were you born?", I sometimes lie.

But there are other often asked questions that I not only don't mind, but that interest me. For example: "Where do your characters come from?" My usual response to that is that they aren't taken from real life and plopped into a story — and that the stories themselves are never a-day-in-the-life versions of things I've actually experienced — or actually experienced that way. Then, depending on how strange the whole process of writing seems to me on that particular day, I add that I don't mistake my life for art, or I say that certain characters can indeed be versions of real people, but that I haven't necessarily met these real people (say, Princess Diana, or Queen Latifah); their secret desires, eccentricities and speech patterns have registered with me from photographs or from items in the tabloids.

In retrospect, I've realized that I've never begun a story because I wanted to reveal something about a character. It's absolutely necessary that I do this, of course, but when I'm working on the first draft, I file that in the back of my mind and proceed to name some hypothetical being who, in my mind, is immediately seen clearly in one respect, standing in a room, or on the beach, or on a lawn. Because I see instantly the character's context — because I understand the visual world surrounding the character — I'm able to know instinctively whether the story is in past or present tense. I pick up ambient sound before I begin to register dialogue (or awkward silence), I squint to see the character's first tiny movements (Oh hell: he smokes), and by then, if I'm lucky, the room in which I write has in effect disappeared, and I'm in the room in which my cigarette smoking man stands. I become a fly on the wall because I don't want to be noticed. My sensibility will inevitably be noticed, but any direct confrontation between myself — because I know myself too well — and the character (or, by this time, characters) could only be counterproductive. Without me there to enact the usual social shuffle (entering with a smile; commenting on the obvious), the character, who may intuit he is being spied on, may be provoked into saying or doing something uncharacteristic, and in those off-moments, of course, people tend to reveal more with their impulsive gestures or their outbursts than they reveal when they are being assiduously observed. My characters, hopefully, are the animated equivalents of out-takes during a portrait shoot. I think of Richard Avedon's portrait of Marilyn Monroe: her eyes closed; an unmistakable aura of sadness surrounding her as she sits picture pretty in her low-cut evening gown. It isn't a definitive photograph, but it's a picture that makes you realize other images must be factored in if you have any interest in getting to the complex truth of the woman. Hereafter, you'll have to superimpose this Marilyn with the better known Marilyn who's reached down to stop her big swirl of skirt from blowing up entirely. And if you retain those polarities, you'll probably be prepared to believe anything you continue to see: Marilyn in a head scarf, golfing; Marilyn with the Kennedy brothers; the fuzzy photograph that recently appeared in a European tabloid that was said to depict Marilyn, naked, face-down in bed, dead.

Where do my characters come from? As quickly as possible, they come into focus as people I both recognize and do not recognize, by which I do *not* mean that a personal friend appears in the story, suddenly dressed in an odd way. But I have to have the same empathetic reaction to the character I would have toward a friend — or toward someone who was going to be a friend; I know, I have noticed, only so much — so the character is likely to be someone who makes me comfortable enough to animate him or her but one who retains enough mystery to make me excitedly uncomfortable about the outcome of his or her life.

Where my characters come from varies from story to story. I think part of the answer is that they come from the same places the people in my life come from: as a small child, I outright invented them; there was a Mr. Mandell, who was going to capture me and put me on a boat to China, whose presence I protested every time the lights went out (My mother said, "Let's get another thought." Where my dialogue comes from — or at least where the really good dialogue comes from — is another story). They come from stories friends tell me about their friends whom I don't know. Sometimes I eventually meet these friends of friends, who inevitably think I'm psychic. They say, "You won't believe this, but the same thing happened to me." They come from what I understand of life by going to the movies and by walking down the street and by befriending new dogs. But this gets too diffuse, I realize. These are the things people say (gesturing in all directions) when they want to suggest they have mastered a great complexity. I could probably make "Where I get my characters from" sound like a mixture of my great common sense, which paradoxically accompanies my (some would say) unsophisticated, or at least self-deprecating, sense of wonder at the world, and the ways of the people therein. I could lie, as I sometimes do about where I was born, and explain their evolution so that it would sound reasonable — meaning, reproducible — because I'm sure people's desire to proceed the same way a published writer proceeds is often the subtext of the "Where do they come from?" question. I could remember to add that I'm somewhat mystical, and that I think some characters have been a sort of cosmic gift. I should also be forthcoming and say that it's often been disquieting, feeling so vulnerable to a character's vicissitudes; they can cause you the same trouble as real life people. Which leads me to the final thing I have to say on the subject of characters.

They've come into my life in the same strange way so many things have. Years ago, when I lived with a bunch of people in Connecticut, we didn't have a key to lock the door in our rented house, so through the years I went back to that house to find, for example, a dead raccoon in the sink with ice cubes dumped over its head (courtesy of the garbage man, who knew one of the people who lived there loved to make road kill stew). One day I encountered the dog catcher eating a sandwich in the kitchen. I don't believe the dog had run away. Another time, after an entire day home alone, I went for the first time into the kitchen and found a young man meditating silently on top of the washing machine. He had hitched from Vermont to Connecticut and gone to the wrong house. I'm married to a man who moved to Charlottesville, VA, for a semester to teach. One month before he left, he caved in to pressure from an acquaintance in New York and called me, having found the one expired phone book that printed my unlisted number. My friends are — to make quick sense of them — "diverse." Some appear months later than expected, hauling caravans of trucks pulling trailers that contain two dogs, four cats, two birds, and a much nose-and-ear-pierced daughter, and getting to Maine just in time to have the whole road show sink in the field across from our house during a summer hurricane. For the eccentrics, I don't have to look far. But if I'm amused in real life, why bother to recast people in fiction? It's the less excessive friends who more often appear, standing in the room holding the cigarette they don't smoke, though as they come into focus I see not a snapshot from life, but an instant collage of what's there and what isn't: my sofa; certainly not a painting I'd want to own; and please, a joke's a joke, but couldn't that Inca flute music be turned down? As he walks across the floor to adjust the volume, the character metamorphoses into a total stranger. In a horror film, I'd hold my breath, but this has happened so many times in stories that I only perk up slightly. Finally: something I'm not even slightly in control of. By the time he gets to the stereo, Mozart is playing, and he has the good sense not to turn it off, but simply to put his head on top of the machine and close his eyes. The character who next walks into the room is bound to understand it all, instantly. I'll just be transcribing her actions. From there, the story unfolds—one hopes on some real trajectory—until the moment when characters who have defined themselves suddenly change. One speaks, saying something out-of-character. The other reacts. The answer is even more unexpected. My stories don't always follow this pattern, of course, but once it's all there—text and subtext and characters who have a life of their own—I get to step in, become a part of the final shaping, because by then I can intuit what's needed to make it work as a story.

In 1979 I wrote a story called "The Burning House." At the end of the story—which I knew was coming because everything else was in place—something happened that astonished me, and that also allowed the story to be completed. The husband and wife, after a strange day of feeding house guests and dealing with their child's anxiety, and the woman's whispered conversations with her lover on the telephone, and all the overwrought house guests generally blowing around like dust stirred by a fan, retire to their bedroom.

"Did you decide what you're going to do after Mark's birthday?" I say.

He doesn't answer me. I touch him on the side, finally.

"It's two o'clock in the morning. Let's talk about it another time."

Yes, please, this story was about to conclude.

"You picked the house, Frank. They're your friends downstairs. I used to be what you wanted me to be."

"They're your friends, too," he says. "Don't be paranoid."

"I want to know if you're staying or going."

This woman is going to persist? The story's almost over.

He takes a deep breath, lets it out, and continues to lie very still. "Everything you've done is commendable," he says. "You did the right thing to go back to school. You tried to do the right thing by finding yourself a normal friend like Marilyn. But your whole life you've made one mistake — you've surrounded yourself with men. Let me tell you something. All men — if they're crazy, like Tucker, if they're gay as the Queen of the May, like Redd Fox, even if they're just six years old — I'm going to tell you something about them. Men think they're Spider-Man and Buck Rogers and Superman. You know what we all feel inside that you don't feel? That we're going to the stars."

He takes my hand. "I'm looking down on all of this from space," he whispers. "I'm already gone."

My characters, who surprise, and enlighten, and dismay me so often, come from familiar worlds with unfamiliar subtexts. Similarly, they are "real" — not made-up — until the very early point in any story when they will not be contained, and then they are transformed so they are beyond my comprehension until the moment something clicks, and then I know what I did not know before, or did not articulate to myself. Inventing characters is for me no different from inventing any day. The best days, though, are the ones that contain real inventions. The days when I write stories.

DAVID FREEMAN

THE SCREENWRITER'S LEXICON

THE NEW YORKER

"So is it a fish out of water or womjep?"
"It's tits 'n' tires. And no sympathy."
"Then pair them up, get M.H.M.E."
"M.B.A.! M.B.A.! You're talking strictly N.A.L.W."
"Sorry. I should think more like Joe."
"Joe? Joe? He doesn't bother with this stuff."

The idea of the unhappy screenwriter is part of Hollywood's mythology. Screenwriters live, famously, in gilded cages, where producers torture them, studio bosses fire them, and actresses ask them where the director is. Many are fallen intellectuals, smarter than the scripts they turn out. Perhaps because irony is not always a useful quality in a Hollywood script, it surfaces in the writers' conversation, which is marked by private references and obscure abbreviations.

Fish out of water: Every few months, another catchphrase surfaces for the sort of script the studios want. It's not anything as simple as "A cop movie is a hit, so let's make another." The task is to identify and reduce to a few words the underlying theme. In "Scent of a Woman," the young man played by Chris O'Donell is a provincial scholarship boy at a fancy prep school—a fish out of water. He accompanies an odd military man, Al Pacino, to the big city—so he's twice out of water, enough to asphyxiate most fish. As in all the fish movies of the last sixty years, he learns to live and flourish.

Womjep: A woman in jeopardy; sometimes called femjep. It's a hardy perennial among movie plots, from "The Perils of Pauline" to "Slumber Party Massacre." The fems in jep were once beautiful and helpless and had torn clothes. They're still beautiful, but now they're often surgeons or architects in torn clothes.

Tits 'n' tires: The sort of movie that responsible adults once felt obligated to condemn. A misunderstood young man would steal a car and drive fast. He slowed down long enough to pick up a young woman who had a compulsion to unbutton her shirt. Today the car thieves are often women and their temporary companions dim-witted drifters with well-developed pectorals. The gender and the era may change, but in Hollywood, cars and chests are inseparable.

Sympathy: Producers and directors want their heros to be sympathetic. This is more complicated than it might seem. Because producers have heard that drama is about change, they want to make sure that change is apparent. If it's a story of youth maturing (always a good bet, considering the age of the audience), chances are a writer will make the youth callow at first. Producers always profess to understand. Then, as surely as the popcorn will be overpriced, they panic when they see those callow beginnings. "More sympathy! More sympathy!" says the producer, sounding like Count Dracula asking for blood. "I wanna love him. Give him a puppy dog! Give him a limp!" "The puppy dog has a limp?" the screenwriter asks. "Hey! I don't know. You're the writer."

M.H.M.E.: More heart, more edge — reduced to initials by writers who have heard it too often. It's the sort of instruction issued by people in authority who haven't any idea what they're talking about but recognize that "Do it again, better" is insufficient. It means, as far as it means anything, to make the emotions larger and the danger greater. "This script needs more heart, more edge," the producer says. "Oh, now I see," the writer says. "Very helpful." "Hey! That's what I'm here for."

M.B.A.: Male-bonding alert. (Nothing to do with a business-school degree.) After the success of the "Lethal Weapon" movies, scripts about unlikely pairs of men who learn to be friends threatened to engulf us all. Screenwriters have learned to warn one another with the anguished cry "M.B.A.!"

N.A.L.W.: Not an A-list writer. This includes almost every screenwriter. The shorthand comes from the now unplugged Writers Guild computer bulletin board (WGA-BBS), where so many abbreviations appeared that a typical screen looked like the first draft of a script about F.D.R. and the New Deal.

Joe: Joe Eszterhas is a hero to a generation of screenwriters, held in esteem not for his scripts — "Basic Instinct" and "Sliver" are recent examples — but for his sales record. He prefers to stay out of development, keeping his own counsel. He usually doesn't take money in advance, and so doesn't have anyone looking over his shoulder. Journalists love to write about how he stood up to Mike Ovitz — a confrontation they tend to paint in Capra-like terms. Screenwriters, who know better, talk only about how Eszterhas sells script after script for a few million dollars a pop without even living in Hollywood.

INGLISH: WRITING WITH AN ACCENT

Tajo, tajo, tajo! tajo, my mackey massa!
O! laud, O! tajo, tajo, tajo!
You work him, mackey massa!
You sweet me, mackey massa!
A little more, my mackey massa!

(Anonymous, work-song recorded by J.B.
Moreton in Jamaica, 1793, *Caribbean Verse*, 3-4).

When I was asked to speak on "Inglish: Writing With an Accent," I applauded the conference organizers for the deconstruction of the word "Inglish." Why? Well, I felt that they did not perceive the participants as victims, that we (the participants) could establish our own power—a power to manipulate this language (English) to our needs.

Tahar Ben Jelloun writes that "[t]he act of speaking is perhaps illusory because it occurs in the language of the Other. . . ." My comprehension of Jelloun's reference is that he has critically placed "the Other" in historically, colonial constructions, where language is colonization and hence colonization is language. For me, this word "Inglish" is far from being an illusion—it is a reality, it is our construct. We have spoken, and we have spoken within an important context! In my opinion, that's an important act. I cannot think of any one who articulates it better than Jelloun when he says "what is most important . . . is not what the mother said, but the fact that she spoke."

As a writer of African descent, I asked myself, what does this mean, writing with an accent? Is it writing out of an ancestral tradition that is central to speech? A synthesis of oral, literary and visual translation? In Africa, for example, symbols are painted on cloth, representing Ghanaian proverbs, sayings and myths. And is this writing with an accent to be considered postmodern or postcolonial writing?

For the past five hundred years books have been written to glorify European culture and many of these are written from an Anglo-European and imperialist perspective. This approach continues to flourish, particularly in institutions and among some writers and scholars. Eurocentrism persists in the "intellectualism" of even the more progressive thinkers. This is the kind of structural and institutional impediment that I must break down in order to create a space for my work. Historically, my ancestors did not sit and wait for institutions to bring about change. People of African descent have had to forge new pathways for themselves; before dub poetry became popular, it was not accepted in the mainstream literary tradition but was viewed as a fringe phenomenon.

I have come to realize that I have to use the vernacular in the manner that I see fit, and that the English language falls into this terrain. The English language is not my enemy. I have the power to use it to my advantage, as did my ancestors, for survival and flexibility. I think that one of the strong points of the British is their understanding of the power of culture and language. In her introduction to the *Penguin Book of Caribbean Verse*, Paula Burnett reminds us of such British characteristics when she writes: "The British never made the mistake of underestimating the importance of language." Upon the arrival of slaves from Africa, they separated those who spoke the same language to prevent any kind of rebellion.

As an African Canadian writer, I am drawing from a painful and complex history of cumulative experiences born out of slavery and colonization and the dispersal of Africans to various parts of what is termed the New World. But in spite of this exploitation and brutality, we have managed to overcome tremendous obstacles in order to create a synthesis of ancient African literary traditions and imperialist literary constructs. Thus Jamaican vernacular is a dynamic marriage of the English and African languages. Louise Bennett's poetry is an excellent example of this marriage. What follows is the last stanza from her poem, "Colonization in Reverse":

> Wat a devilment a Englan!
> Dem face war an brave de worse,
> But we wonderin how dem gwine stan
> Colonizin in reverse.
>
> (*Carribean Verse*, 33)

This poetry is relevant to those comprehensively engaged in what Burnett describes as a "search for forms of creative cohabitation," which allow for "the assertion of cultural self without the denial of that assertion to others, and the sharing of as much as can be shared."

For me, the Jamaican vernacular was not taught or encouraged in my school days. It was not spoken by me or my peers. Yet even though it was viewed as an inferior langauge, I was very interested in it and was illuminated when it was spoken, especially during the times when I went to pantomime.

But I will admit that it wasn't until 1985 that I penned my first non-standard poem using the Jamaican vernacular. It wasn't a very easy poem to write. As a matter of fact, I was apprehensive. I wasn't sure that I could translate the music, the rhythm into a vigorous and meaningful language and maintain the strong voice that I was hearing and feeling. Writing this poem opened a significant pathway for me as a writer. I was no longer a silent listener and observer of this language. I was now an active participant. I will now conclude with a poem from my book *No Contingencies*:

A PRETTY BABY GIRL IN A DA NURSERY

Mi 'ave a baby girl
She dah weight six pounds two oz
Mi a com' out of hospital pon thursday

Mi nuh 'ave no place to go
And only a dolla' to mi name

Mi dah call de pickney father
'im sey
Him comin to see mi
Mi nuh se 'im yet

One whole 'ear now
Mi dah go together
Yu no mis
'im left and' go married Doris two mon' now
'ere mi a lay

With only a dolla' to mi name
With only a dolla' to mi name
'nd a pretty baby girl
In a di nursery
'nd a pretty baby girl
In a di nursery

Works Cited

Bennett, Louise. "Colonization in Reverse." In *The Penguin Book of Caribbean Verse in English*. Ed. Paula Burnett. New York: Penguin, 1986. 32-3.

Black, Ayanna. *No Contingencies*. Toronto: Williams/Wallace, 1986. 16.

Burnett, Paula. Introduction to *The Penguin Book of Caribbean Verse*, xxiii-lxiv.

Jelloun, Tahar Ben. *Harrouda*. Cited in "Travel, Representation and Difference, or how can one be a Parisian." By Elizabeth Mudimbe-Boyi. *Research in African Literature* 23:3 (Fall 1992). 25-39.

BEN NYBERG

WHY STORIES FAIL

LITERARY MAGAZINE REVIEW

A few years ago I set down my impressions of why stories succeed, or at least what makes literary magazine editors (like myself) take and publish the stories they do. The resulting essay, "The Serious Business of Choosing Literary Fiction," took up only seven pages in the 1986 *Fiction Writer's Market*. I could cover so large a subject in so few pages because I wasn't trying to do much more than identify the qualities and describe the effects that nearly all well-crafted short fiction shares.

For all their diversity, successful stories, like Tolstoy's happy families, have a lot in common—to quote myself: Honesty, Efficiency, Complexity, Authority, Originality. Whereas every single unsuccessful fiction is "unhappy" in its own unique way, so that even listing all the separate reasons short stories fail becomes a hopeless task. Still, after reading a thousand-plus story manuscripts every year for twenty-five years, I've come to recognize some family resemblances among the failed faces in the mixed crowd of hopefuls I screen daily, enough of them that it should be possible to sort most of the specific flaws by kin or kind into larger categories of style and strategy and perhaps come up with some generalizations that may help writers avoid a few of the most common pitfalls of their chosen genre.

Of course any system of classification is bound to be flawed by blind caprice and unwitting bias. When the question is how to codify something as complicated as the whole range of error in handling the grammar and rhetoric of fiction, the task is formidable. I may be thought foolhardy even to try it. But I proceed in the assurance that I seek to propose neither a formulaic paradigm for writers nor a Procrustean set of standards for editors. Rather my intent is to lay out as clearly and completely as possible what I've learned in my editing career about what makes stories fail, in the conviction that seeing what's wrong must always be the first step toward getting it right.

Since I can't, in 1992, improve on those criteria of success I proposed back in 1986, I'll use them—or rather the *lack* of them—to outline the causes of failure as well. But as successful stories all share the virtue of winning the races they run, and many unsuccessful ones seem to drop out long before they can break their finish-line tape, I'll also look at deficiencies in terms of what stage in a story's progress flaws normally appear and take their toll. Some problems, like genetic birth defects, date back to a story's conception and keep it from running its race at all, whereas others—equally crucial but more subtle—don't show up till the run is almost over and victory seems all but certain.

So I've taken the familiar three phase division of a story into beginning (exposition), middle (complication/crisis), and end (resolution/denouement), added a "pre-story" fourth division, and considered each division in the light of my five basic criteria, which gives me twenty categories to consider, each with its special pitfalls. To clarify focus I've also sorted my remarks into subsections labeled according to fiction's traditional elements: setting, plot, character, and theme. Marginal extracts from actual letters I've sent writers over the years complete the format.

HOW STORIES FAIL
BEFORE THEY START

To begin at the beginning, let's consider how stories can fail even before they get going. Impossible? Hardly. In fact, probably more stories are disabled by mistakes during advance planning, by conceptual errors made before the writer pens a single line than at any other stage of construction.

Pre-Story Lapses in Honesty

By honesty in fiction I mean knowing what one is writing about and writing only about what one knows. Most of the world's great fiction is grounded, one way or another, in real life. Yet not all knowledge is life-based. It is possible through research to learn enough about places and times outside one's own autobiographical history to make their other-worldly settings feel as familiar and "lived-in" as first-hand experience. Obviously historical fiction requires writers to reach beyond their "natural" time frame.

Even more so do the futuristic speculations of s-f writers. No library has research materials on alien life forms, history yet to happen. True, this only makes the task of becoming knowledgeable more interesting: s-f writers learn about their worlds by creating them. Not quite from scratch, be to sure. Frank Herbert had earth ecology to work from when he was building *Dune*. And George Orwell had a grim post-WWII view of fascism to help him depict *1984*. The point is, s-f writers are no freer than others to make it up as they go along. Just as surely as authors of "autobiographical" sto-

Dear ----,
We'd like to believe what you ask us to see here, but you've got to see it first.

Dear ----,
A wild adventure, but it just didn't take us along.

Dear ----,
We respect your need to catch the reader's eye, but readers need more than rapid eye movement to keep them interested.

Dear ----,
Life on other worlds has to be different from life on earth, but the differences must mean something to earthly readers if you're going to tell them as a story.

Dear ----,
Your alien world is spooky and zany, but without cause and effect, it's just not possible to lay out an earth-relevant plot.

Dear ----,
Sorry. You just didn't take us into your world. You seemed to be discussing what happened rather than describing it.

Dear ----,
Interesting enough story idea, but the presentation is so detached and remote and uninvolved that you don't seem to have any stake in how it all comes out.

Dear ----,
Ingenious scenario, delightfully quirky narrator, but you just don't make any space for it all to happen in.

Dear ----,
It may happen in a desert, but it can't happen in a void.

Dear ----,
The "Paris" of your story is pretty well documented, but the data has a travel-brochure feel to it, as if you hadn't ever been there in person.

Dear ----,
Why set your story in Greece? Nothing occurs that couldn't just as well happen in Peoria.

ries, they're responsible for the validity of what they record.

Which is what fictive honesty comes down to: making so "real" an "eye-witness" report of what you "see" and "hear" that readers get a feel for what being there was like. So what matters, finally, isn't whether the events of writers' accounts are real, but whether those events "happen" for their readers. A writer who believes what he sees and brings that sureness of vision to his readers is being honest.

So how, specifically, do writers fall short of honesty in the planning stage of stories?

Setting

Surprisingly often, writers seem to give no thought whatsoever to where the action of a story is to take place. Instead of imagining a complete context with solid ground for their people to walk on, they content themselves with putting a character in motion who can only perish from a lack of breathable air. Setting is a story's life-support system, and without it everything dies.

When it isn't entirely ignored, setting is sometimes daubed in dutifully but without conviction, by writers who seem to know that it's supposed to be useful, but whose hastily painted backdrops merely force the characters to act out their scenes on an amateur-hour stage. The quality of life in a story can't exceed the quality of its sustaining environment; to cut corners on setting is to degrade the whole picture.

Finally, just as setting can be under-conceived and executed, it is also possible (though this happens less often) for setting to be over-deliberated to the point that its use becomes suspect. Some writers persist in ignoring Ruskin's famous warning against the "pathetic fallacy" (portraying natural forces as responding in sympathy to human events, e.g., rain = Heaven weeping at someone's death). But obtrusive settings need not be "empathic" to be manipulative, hence dishonest. Except for allegory, where visible action is supposed to serve symbolic sense, setting should stay modestly in the background, not push forward to guide readers' understanding or interpret the author's message.

Character

Dishonesty in conceiving characters is one of the most common planning errors story writers make. And it's a mistake made by many who ought to know better. I myself should have known better, even thirty-some years ago, when I concocted a flimsy high school romance featuring a bespectacled goofball intellectual who falls for a devastatingly cute cheerleader, and sent it off to *Good Housekeeping* as proof that I could do better stuff than their readers were used to getting. My characters were cardboard cutouts, my story a travesty of real-life drama, a mockery of true feeling, and my reward was a well-deserved non-personalized rejection slip.

Such unconvincing characters are usually a result of thinking in generic rather than specific terms. The hero of my silly story had no individual personality because I hadn't bothered to think about him as a person. He was only a function, a means to an end, a stereotype nerd, a big brain drunk with infatuation.

Dear ----,
The weather in your story is too heavy, especially when it tries to clue us in on how to understand Donna's motives.

Dear ----,
We appreciate your desire to give this "Old West" saga the sand-in-the-eye feel of 19th-century Tombstone; but setting laid on this thick is pure mud in the eye of anyone trying to watch the action.

Dear ----,
Probably there are "real" people like these characters, and maybe you know what makes them tick. But unless you let us in on it, they're nothing but so many "scary" Halloween "Costume goblins."

Dear ----,
If you want us to care about and respect your main character in the end, you have to care about and respect him from the beginning. As is, you don't seem to take him seriously till you've already turned him into a cliché.

Dear ----,
Poor Jake acts like a windup toy man that walks off a cliff only because "somebody" set him down and pointed him that way. If he did his own thinking, he might not obey orders.

Dear ----,
But *why* is Leon such a woman-hating swine? Only to give readers a character to hate?

Dear ----,
Your title character is a "femme fatale," but does she have to be "dumb blonde" too? Makes it too easy for you to push her into cheap no-win scrapes.

Dear ----,
Feels like plot leading character to us, which always gives a story a rigged, "predestined" quality.

Dear ----,
Of course life's full of disappointments, but this story reads like a stacked deck. Your "hero" is subjected to Job-like ordeals, but for all the pain you inflict on him, he doesn't learn much and neither do we.

All I was after was a picturesque contrast; I didn't really care whether or not he or his cheerleader heroine had any feelings that might disturb the easy flow of a nifty little tale. It wasn't *their* story, after all, it was *mine*. Such is the error of prideful dishonesty.

But many a more famous writer than I has committed this sin. No need to name names here, just consider all the sleazy "pot-boiler" bestsellers cranked out by reputable authors who either knew better or ought to have. I'm not saying writers shouldn't want to earn money. I *am* saying that bad practice is bad practice, especially when name authors stoop to pander. Because they can get away with it, they cause great harm by encouraging crowds of would-be get-rich-quick imitators to waste time trying their hands at the same sort of tripe.

But what makes such fiction "character-flawed"? Actually, it's both character- and plot-flawed, but the plot errors usually stem from faulty character conception. Years ago I read a very bad novel by Mary Elizabeth Braddon titled *Rupert Godwin*. I now recall little of the wild story line, but it did give me enduring evidence of how devastating an error it is to send a character off on an assignment he's not equipped to tackle. If a mission really is impossible, the story won't sell because readers won't buy it.

Put another way, one of the defining qualities of dramatic tragedy is that it presents a situation that tests the weak spot ("Achilles' heel") of its hero. Thus, Othello would have no trouble coping with Hamlet's problems, and vice versa. But the power of tragedy derives from our sense that, were circumstances just slightly different or our hero's psycho-emotional makeup altered only marginally, the heroic fall would be averted. In other words, the hero's "failure" is the story's intended point. Had it happened by accident, merely because the writer neglected to give his character the strengths or talents needed to cope effectively with the challenges he faces, that would be exactly the sort of planning error I mean.

Characters are sometimes forced into unnatural behavior by writers who are out to prove a point, take revenge, or just vent frustrations. Of course story writers are teachers (even at times preachers) with deeply held beliefs whose fictions convey strong value statements, and they have every right to employ any character they need to tell their tale effectively. But the godlike power to create people carries the equally large responsibility to understand them, to present them as fairly and compassionately as possible. To understand all may not quite be to forgive all, but honest writers always *try* to forgive. Certainly they never treat any of their characters as straw monsters whose only job is to terrify and/or be blown away, or straw wimps and fools who live only to be bullied and humiliated.

So I deny the existence of real, live monsters? Not at all. In life most things are possible, many of them not very interesting. Because it's "real," life may be forgiven some dullness, but fiction can't afford to be dull or pointless. So fiction's successful ogres are its Scrooges, Raskolnikovs, Ahabs—depraved and tormented souls whose spiritual night journeys we watch with a personal involvement born of recognition that somehow or

Dear ----,
Zoe's misfortunes all result from either incredibly bad luck or her own unbelievable stupidity—both of which you seem to inflict on her.

Dear ----,
When Ned gets worked up, he starts spouting such batty claptrap he might as well carry a sign saying "Don't believe me—I'm a wild-eyed radical!"

Dear ----,
Why make Doug such a pushover? Marge could get the better of a smarter cad, so why not let her win a better fight?

Dear ----,
This would be lots more gripping if you gave us something scarier than a freak-show ogre to worry about.

Dear ----,
We print psychological thrillers, but not "situational suspense drama." Even by category horror (Stephen King) standards, your grisly night stalker seems under-motivated to "justify" it in human terms.

Dear ----,
We don't have to love your protagonist, but he needs to have a "nature" human enough for us to relate to.

Dear ----,
Your wild and crazy monologue is amusing, but we get no clue to where this guy is coming from or where he thinks he's taking us.

Dear ----,
Earl keeps telling us he's not insane, and since he's got an author vouching for him we're ready to believe it, but then he goes on not making sense.

Dear ----,
Interesting, but you direct our attention to the abnormalities that divide her from us rather than the qualities she shares with us.

other we share their struggles. The totally, irredeemably evil monster holds no real interest for human readers because its motives don't compute in human terms. A Bad Terminator android is scary; but, lacking the complexity of human motivation, it can't become a truly interesting character.

So even monsters need something driving them more than wicked hearts. However deep are his profligates' or philanderers' villainy, a good writer will explain such behavior well enough to "justify" it in human terms. Criminals' crimes need not be excused, nor their souls redeemed, but an honest story will clarify the reasoning even of sociopaths like Poe's "Tell-Tale Heart" narrator or O'Conner's Misfit in "A Good Man Is Hard to Find."

Which leads to another all-too-common abuse of writer's "license": copping a plea on the basis of insanity. However fair a defense it may be in the real world, it's nothing but a dodge in fiction's court. It's the central difference between life and art: life must acknowledge mental derangement that we mortals can't explain, whereas fiction's "madness" always has its "method." If Hamlet be truly insane, rather than pretending madness as part of a shrewd revenge strategy, his moves are deprived of calculation (and interest!) and his final triumph is reduced to no more than a random shot in the dark, pure fluke. The fictional author of "Diary of a Madman" comes unglued before our eyes, but Gogol's artistry lets readers make sense of even his craziest outbursts.

The bottom line on character invention: people in fiction must have intelligible, supportable reasons for what they do and say, which is possible only if their behavior is motivated by factors a reader can understand and verify from evidence in the story. Unlike flesh-and-blood humans, story personae, however weird, must behave in ways that make some kind of sense; if they don't, their "mystery" stays unsolved, unsolvable, pointless.

Plot

As noted above, many faulty plots are caused by trying to force characters to play out a script they are unqualified for. But of course plot doesn't always follow character, and when it leads it can sometimes take characters for quite a ride. Of particular concern is the plot idea that makes impossible demands on its characters. It may be said that, by this rule, many a famous story premise would have been doomed in advance to certain failure. A man wakes up and finds himself turned into a cockroach? Come on, get real! Or how about basing a novella-length story on the idea that a man wastes his whole life waiting for some event to pounce on him, and doesn't even notice when it bites him on the leg (Henry James's "The Beast in the Jungle")? Don't these scenarios all but guarantee failing stories?

Yes, all but. If I received query letters about either of them as possible material for the magazine I edit, I doubt I'd be interested. I can even imagine myself groaning over the first sentence of Kafka's "Metamorphosis," knowing that I was about to suffer through a hopelessly stupid story. But genius has a way of proving rules by violating them. For every successful tour de force achieved by breaking rules, thousands of experiments fail. Those

Dear ----,
The geyser of disjunctive revelation that spews from your narrator may be meant to fit together, but it was too incoherent for us to follow.

Dear ----,
Maybe, if you had a whole novel to deal with all the issues your plot poses your characters, they might be up to their job.

Dear ----,
It's not enough to startle readers; they expect some food for thought as well.

Dear ----,
We can follow the events of your story, but not the motivation of your characters.

Dear ----,
It takes daring to try something this difficult, and genius to succeed. You come close, but a miss is still a miss.

Dear ----,
We admired the well-decorated corridors of your plot, but ended up feeling that there was more glitter than gold in the story.

Dear ----,
The machinery of your plot is so elaborate that it can't help but draw attention to itself, and once we notice it the illusion of reality is gone.

Dear ----,
Verdi wrote a good opera called *The Force of Destiny*, but in a short story fatalism is usually a recipe for melodrama.

Dear ----,
Serious plots are more than obstacle courses improvised ad hoc by authors intent on keeping the action going.

who defy the odds should be aware of the risks.

Then too, Kafka and James didn't come up with these ideas just to prove they could pull a fast one. They were master craftsmen with a keen awareness of their art's demands who chose story materials not because they were flashy, but because they could be grounded in theme, so that both character and plot obey the dictates of thesis. Those determined to run the risks associated with "incredible" tales should know that theme-powered fiction, being cousin to allegory, does stand a better chance of surviving ventures into the absurd or the surreal.

Plots can also be "well-made" to the point of dishonesty. To be sure, fiction is artifice, and all storylines are accordingly conjectural narrative schemes. But some schemes are so rigid they turn characters into marbles rolling and bumping their way along a set of pre-cut grooves so deep nobody could conceivably get off track.

This sort of "idiot plot" is beautifully illustrated by the cliché film chase in which someone in a car tries to run down someone on foot. In order to make the scene last, two things must happen: 1) the car must not catch up with the runner; 2) the runner must not outrun the car. In order to achieve both these ends, it's necessary to put severe restrictions on both runner and driver. The driver must drive so as to appear to be really trying to catch the runner, and the runner must not run anywhere that a car can't follow. The result is a thoroughly dishonest piece of plotting: runner runs only in streets, parking lots and other open places; driver makes his car roar and buck frantically but without ever closing distance on the fleeing runner.

So most dishonest plot-planning comes down to thinking up adventures that overtax a character's ability or will to accomplish what's asked of him. He must do what he can't (in some cases, what nobody could) or what no one of sound mind would agree to do. But sometimes plot ideas are more innocently dishonest: writers often undermine their credibility by getting historical facts wrong or out of order (anachronism) or contravening established physical or biological laws, or casually contradicting themselves (scrambling natural time by having corn ripen in October), forgetting that a character did something (like walk to a party) that prevents his doing something else (like driving home in his car), etc. Gaffes like these may not seem serious, but for the reader who notices them they can easily destroy a story's illusion of reality. At the least they say that an author isn't really watching his story unfold.

Theme

As noted earlier, theme-dominant fiction leans toward allegory, is by nature more abstract, more overtly symbolic, more concerned about subtextual meaning than is ordinary garden-variety mimetic fiction. But writers of theme stories sometimes get so caught up in "message" they forget that they still need to show as well as tell. No matter how thesis-driven, fiction never "sells direct" in the manner of essays, always presents meaning obliquely, implicitly, for readers to infer.

Ironically, it's usually when writers work too

Dear ----,
You seem more concerned with thwarting Dave's progress toward his goal than with understanding why he wants to reach it.

Dear ----,
You seem to want us to believe that John is really a skilled fly fisherman, yet you commit so many errors in describing basic technical skills that we began to wonder if it was deliberate, and if so, why.

Dear ----,
For a 1960s "period piece," your story contains far too many slang terms from more recent decades (and several bits of consumer goods as well).

Dear ----,
Your story arrives like a Delphic pronouncement, abstract and lacking clear contextual references, leaving us to puzzle away at its riddles as best we can.

Dear ----,
You make your point forcefully and cogently, but the story feels over-argued, pushed at to make its own way.

Dear ----,
Ben sounds suspiciously like a "mouthpiece." If you want us to "buy" what he says, better not let him say it.

Dear ----,
This isn't so much a story as a dramatized debate with Ms. Pro and Mr. Con duking it out for ten bloody rounds.

Dear ----,
If you really want to write tracts, maybe you ought to switch to propaganda's natural essay genre rather than trying to twist fiction to your ends.

hard at making their intended statements clear and emphatic that they lose their grip on the dramatic illusion necessary to sustain their case. In their desire to spell things out so unambiguously no reader will mistake them, they may be tempted to thrust a more-or-less explicit message into the story's text, sometimes even putting wise words in the mouth of a "spokesman" character—whether he can speak them or not. The impression left may be earnest and intense, but it always has a hollow, unconvincing ring to it, because the writer has resorted to "special pleading" in support of a shaky argument.

Strange to say, one of the most common failings of theme fiction is thematic insincerity. Stories by writers with a point to prove might be expected to burn with even greater zeal than most, but in fact theme fiction seems to be the medium of choice for those who simply want to impress the world with their ability. Like my story mentioned earlier, condescendingly written to show the editors of *Good Housekeeping* what they were missing, too many apprentice-level theme stories have an attitude problem. Most of the time what makes such scenarios dishonest is that their authors are trying to argue for (or against) causes that they lack the knowledge to discuss. I must have rejected hundreds of stories that were nothing but shallow diatribes against abortion, capital punishment, police brutality, political corruption, spouse abuse, and other hot topics by writers more concerned with attracting attention to themselves than stirring reader concern about anything.

Sadly, sincerity is itself no guarantee of thematic honesty. Often a theme story author's subjective dedication to a pet cause actually spawns other sorts of dishonesty: selective documentation, which gives the argument an unconvincing slant; distorted evidence, rotten apples that can spoil a whole barrel of sound ones; and skewed logic, which turns authors into con artists.

It's probably fair to say of theme stories that, though they are the rarest of fiction's usual birds, they are also the ones most likely to crash and burn. Taking flight from a perch removed from visible reality, they seem to meet with more problems in fictional aerodynamics.

Dear ----,
We approve the passionate commitment you bring to your writing, but the "blood in your eye" keeps you from seeing your characters and their story fairly and truly enough to make us trust your account.

JAMES FENTON

MISTAKES PEOPLE MAKE ABOUT POETRY

THE NEW YORK REVIEW OF BOOKS

Writing from Ravenna to Thomas Moore in 1821, Byron said that he could "never get people to understand that poetry is the expression of an excited passion, and that there is no such thing as a life of passion any more than a continuous earthquake or an eternal fever." And he added as an afterthought: "Besides, who would ever *shave* themselves in such a state?" It's worth hearing this from Byron of all people—Byron who could fill his days with riding, lovemaking, and drinking and then sit down late at night in an excited passion and pen an extraordinarily large number of stanzas. But Byron's standards in passion were high. There was no such thing as a *life* of passion, and there was no such thing as a *life* of poetry.

Ravenna, a remote place even now, was an exceedingly remote place in those days. Byron's exile—a thing lived through, it seems to us, with so much passion—was partly a matter of getting away from his admirers as well as his critics, from those who expected on meeting him to encounter the original Childe Harold. Byron was not like Childe Harold—or rather he was not *always* like Childe Harold. This was the mistake people made about his poetry.

If he was right about poetry being the product of an excited passion, the consequences for the way we regard our lives as poets can be both liberating and depressing. Byron was the most prolific of poets and one of the most successful commercially, but the idea that poetry might be a career was absolutely alien to him—alien to him, of course, as an aristocrat, but alien to him, anyway, as a figure of his time. Indeed, careerism in poetry is a very recent, perhaps postwar phenomenon.

To earn the title of poet in previous centuries it was enough that one had written *a* poem. Nobody thought that Gray, who made his reputation on a dozen poems, was any less the poet for that. Even today Dr. Johnson's claim to the title poet rests on a couple of satires, *London* and *The Vanity of Human Wishes* (the tragedy *Irene* having ducked out of sight). But either one of those satires would have been sufficient to validate the claim.

This is not to imply that the poets of previous centuries were easily satisfied with their achievements, that they never yearned to go on churning the stuff out, that they never felt blocked as writers. Nor is it to imply that they had no ulterior motive when they wrote, no further object in view. Indeed they did have an object, about which they were notably more frank than we are. Their object was Fame.

But their object was not a *career*. You have to go back a long way, and rummage through some quite obscure poetry, before you find a careerism of the kind that is common today. Court poets were careerists, no doubt, if they were writing poems in order to secure a stipend—the kind of thing, for instance, encouraged at the court of Ferrar, long disquisitions on the future glories of the House of Este. But most poetry written at court was of a different, more casual kind. Maybe the occasional sonnet helped oil the machine, but the courtier's life did not depend on his producing a slim volume every three years. Walter Raleigh was not beheaded because he'd been unable to find a publisher, because he'd been turned down by Knopf and Random House and Farrar Straus. But the career plight of the modern American poet obliged to protect his tenure by dutifully collecting up everything that he has written in the past year, *and everything that has been written about him*, to send off to some authority who will then assess the output—this is a relatively new humiliation for the writer and it is a menace to art.

But even without it, there is something in the spirit of the times that will tend to lure poets into overproduction—a vanity encouraging us to write for the bookshelf. Oh, to produce a nice big volume, or a *series* of volumes, something that could hold its head up high alongside the collected speeches of Kim Il Sung or Todor Zhivkov, something that could only possibly be published by arrangement with the late Robert Maxwell.

This tendency toward gigantism is a lingering part, oddly enough, of the Romantic legacy. Most poets I know, if offered the choice between being Catullus or being Victor Hugo, imagine they would choose to be Catullus—short, elegant, and to the point, unlikely to waste anyone's time. However, like those people who supposedly set out last April to vote Labour but who found as they left the polling booth that they had actually voted Tory, at the very moment when our hands were reaching out to tick the Catullus box that inexplicable something would occur. We would plump for the comfortingly big *oeuvre*, the thing that would give us an outward and visible assurance that there was an achievement there, even if it was explained that a great deal of this *oeuvre* would remain forever unread. We'd prefer to *read* Catullus, but to *be* Victor Hugo.

The reason for this is that we lack reassurance, and this lack is a necessary part of our condition as poets. We are the very opposite of performing artists, who, except in very peculiar cases, will *know* whether or not they have succeeded in their art. (The reason why Florence Foster Jenkins's case remains celebrated is that it was so unusual for a singer not to be aware that she was absolutely frightful.) It would be very odd to go to a concert hall and discover that the pianist on offer *wasn't any good at all*, in the sense that he couldn't actually play the piano. But in poetry this is an experience we have learned to take in our stride.

There are no forensic tests for poetry, in the sense that there are for musicians. It's obvious that if I can't pass Grade Five there's no point in booking the Wigmore Hall. But who can prescribe the skills I must achieve before I publish a poem? Who is to devise the exercises, the examinations? No doubt it is depressing enough to be dedicated to an art such as music or dance, which puts you through a long, rigorous training and then at a certain point may say: Sorry, this is as far as you get—this is your level. But at least within a certain broad band of knowing, you know where you are. A poet like Auden, on the other hand—a poet so abundantly stocked with ideas—claimed never to finish a poem without the dreadful sense that he would never write again. My own experience is quite the opposite: when I am lucky enough to complete a poem, I imagine that I shall now be able to repeat the trick two or three times over. It is only later, as the wake of the excited passion recedes, that I realize I'm in for another long wait.

Some artists are blessed with the incontrovertible knowledge that they are working. However much they may fret about the standard of their work, they know they are spending so much time a day practicing, modeling, sketching, whatever. But if poetry is the expression of an excited passion, the idea of practicing seems somehow foreign to the art.

So how do I know whether I'm working or not? For most poets the answer must surely be that we will spend most of our lives not working, in the ostensible sense of putting down lines on paper. All that we can hope is that the lives we lead will be compatible with the writing of poetry, that with any luck they will stimulate us to write. It may be that a poet will find a thing to do which seems to be the equivalent of practicing scales—going for long walks or pacing up and down the garden, like Wordsworth—but whatever it is, it will always have the status of a Thing Which Seems To Do The Trick. That is the most we can hope for.

We work in an atmosphere of bemusement. I knew one Englishman who got a good start in poetry—magazine publication, slim volume, and then even a prize. The further it went, the less happy this guy became with his success, since he really had never had the foggiest notion what he was up to. He didn't understand his own poems, and he didn't understand the praise that came his way.

So after a while, seeing that the whole thing was in danger of ending in tears, he rather bravely gave up writing poetry. I won't presume to add that he lived happily ever after, because I suppose there would always be, at the back of your mind, a feeling that all poets are con artists, and you might as well be in it for what you can get out of it. But my impression was that he was reasonably happy not to continue through life with this mysterious feeling of having wandered into the wrong party.

A young student, an American, put the matter to me like this: if it were a choice between achieving a normal, healthy, well-adjusted life on the one hand, and becoming a poet on the other, he would rather lead the normal, healthy, well-adjusted life. And this made things very much easier between us since he was, if a choice had to be made, much more suited to normality than he was to poetry. In fact, although I did not say so, if he'd just given up his very fast motorbike and perhaps eaten a bit more fresh fruit, he could have had his whole life's ambition then and there. In poetry, he did not know what he was doing, but this *not knowing* was not a matter of surrendering to instinct, adventuring into the unknown. The problem was that, step by step and ineluctably, he had been persuaded to eliminate from his definition of poetry anything that might have made it identifiable as such, until he had been left with only one thing to hang on to — the notion that poetry "used heightened language." What constituted heightened language was hard to define, since obvious heightening agents such as rhythm and rhyme had already been specifically excluded.

He was melancholy and incurious. Nothing in his education so far had persuaded him to take any profound interest in the existing poetry of his own language, the language which he shared with so many nations and cultures. He lived within easy access of bookshops and libraries, he had read the poetry of the various people who had taught him poetry, and he had listened to the work of other members of his group. But beyond this rather limited milieu his curiosity did not extend. The poetry of past centuries antagonized him, as did anything (he was from the American Midwest) that could be described as East Coast.

Put this way, the student sounds rather a dim case, but this was not entirely so. On the subject of his favorite music, and song in particular, he was lively, informative, and curious. His taste had its own natural authority. So much so that I began to wonder whether his education in poetry might not be to blame. His education had attempted to knock the poetry out of him but his natural taste had preserved an area that was education-free, protected by having been psychologically split off. If he was writing a song, he knew perfectly well the kind of thing he was after, even if he could not achieve it. But he never associated the song side with the poetry side of his life. Poetry perhaps overawed him, but he didn't want anything to happen that might reduce its vacuous augustness. He didn't want a hint of lightness, for instance, or humor, in a poem. I don't think he really wanted it to be interesting. He preferred to keep it a bit awesome and a bit empty.

He was, in short, a victim of the tyranny of free or "open" form, but I should like to think the difference between us was not a matter of formalism (or neoformalism) versus free verse. That might have seemed to him and his group to be part of the problem when we argued. But I do not think the cause of poetry should be hijacked aboard the neoconservative gravy train. Nor do I think there is any sense in an attempt to turn back the clock, or to return to imagined premodernist values. There is modernism in the history of everything we write. Understanding it and benefitting from it is a part of our education as poets. But we live in a period rapidly becoming as remote from that of Eliot and Pound as theirs was from the Romantics—even if, in tribute to modernism, people still talk about it as something that has just happened. My bemused midwestern poetry group thought that modernism was a matter of readjusting our attitude to art after Hiroshima and the concentration camps. They plumped for the wrong world war.

The neoconservative take on all this, the reassertion of "values," is an uncandid attempt to enlist poets in a political cause. The concern is not for the well-being of poetry itself, but to persuade the poets to come along to lend any aura they might have to the neoconservative event. Neoformalism is a queer thing. It has a tendency to champion forms of poetry which, in the premodernist age, were only of marginal interest. All those sestinas, *ballades*, and villanelles so beloved of Auden and Empson can hardly be of the essence. They seem to attract the neoformalist because, when it comes to the teaching of poetry, they help provide the missing forensic test mentioned earlier. Maybe they could stand in as scales, as arpeggios; the sestina is Grade Five, the villanelle Grade Six, and so forth. Maybe they could be the things we oblige our students to practice every day: the Petrarchan sonnet could be the medicine ball, and we'd keep in shape by chucking it about for ten minutes every morning. But then again, maybe not. I think Pound liked the Troubadour forms because they struck him as fresh, not because they smacked of the gym or schoolroom.

Yeats told the Irish poets to learn their trade, which is fine as long as those Irish poets don't come away with the idea that poetry is a *trade*. Learn your craft, laddy! Yes please, I should like to learn my craft, but I came under the impression that poetry was an art, and that an art was more than a craft. A poetry workshop may be a fine thing. But to talk of a *workshop* is merely a well-meaning attempt at demystification. Poetry is not fashioned on an anvil or thrown on a potter's wheel. These are only metaphors, and we do danger to the art if we talk of it always in craft terms.

Indeed, one might question the motive of some of this demystification. A whole culture has grown up around the idea of poetry workshops, and it might be worth stepping back from time to time and asking: Am I being conned or am I conning myself about these groups? Am I here under a false prospectus? We are all familiar with those advertisements which claim that a publisher is looking for poems. Ian Hamilton once investigated the con: you sent in your poems and received what purported to be encouraging criticism; you were also encouraged to publish, and to pay for the pleasure of doing so. At the end of the process your work appeared as part of an anthology — an anthology of you and your fellow dupes, an anthology no one else would see.

Babies are not brought by storks, and poets are not produced by workshops. It's worth keeping these truths in mind to avoid disappointment. A workshop can be many things: an encounter group, with all the rewarding and devastating possibilities that implies; a glee club; a mutual entertainment; a reading circle; a matter of joint research. Where it develops into a menace is where it is considered as something to be added to your CV, and those most at risk from this menace are the people obsessed with extending their poetic CVs. Look: all is well, I've acquired some more qualifications, I've added another inch to my stature as a poet!

And this adding of inches to the CV is bound to disappoint, as it becomes clear that the CV is moving in one direction and the career, mysteriously, in another. Until eventually my CV implies that I'm just about to become Goethe, and yet I have to admit that not even my cat believes this. The mistake was to think of poetry as a career. For if poetry is the product of an excited passion, and if there is no such thing as a life of passion, a continuous earthquake or an eternal fever, how much less likely is it that there would be a *career* of passion? If it is liberating to be told that a single poem can earn you the title of poet, there remains the depressing catch that we will never know whether we have written that single poem.

Plaudits are fun. Neglect is miserable. But we shall never be able to tell either from the plaudits or from the neglect whether we have come anywhere near the fulfillment of our aim. Keats died under the impression of failure. Mrs. Felicia Hemans (her gold-tooled, leather-bound volumes selling like hot cakes) had probably been lulled, one way or another, into a sense of significant achievement. What a shock she must have got looking down from Heaven or meeting the dead Emily Dickinson there. Such, you might say, are the risks of this vocation.

One thinks of Philip Larkin, beginning adult life with the over-riding ambition to become a novelist. The poetry was what he wrote when the novels wouldn't flow. And when that flow stopped altogether he was left with the dismaying realization that he must look elsewhere, he must rely on poetry, his second string. But in the meantime, since the poetry was not likely to come in a torrent, there was all that life to be led, all that consciousness to be got through, and death to be faced at the end of it all — and all this to be endured without the common consolations of a shared existence. A childless life with depression for a muse. Not exactly a course which one would rush to sign on for, if it were offered, and the prospectus were clear.

NATALIA RACHEL SINGER

NONFICTION IN FIRST PERSON, WITHOUT APOLOGY

CREATIVE NONFICTION

In his introduction to the 1989 *The Best American Essays*, Geoffrey Wolff tells a story about how, in writing an essay on *King Lear* as a young boarding school boy, he could not help but narrate some of his own misunderstandings with his *Duke of Deception* father to illustrate his sympathy with Cordelia. Wolff's teacher wrote the customary "who cares?" in red ink on his essay, insisting, as we were all taught, that when one writes nonfiction, it is necessary to "take facts in, quietly manipulate them behind an opaque scrim, and display them as though the arranger never arranged." Reading Wolff's story made me think of my childhood in Cleveland, and my decision, at the ripe age of five, to devote my life to becoming a writer. I remember thinking, as I watched my parents' marriage dissolve, and I stayed up late staring out the window at the acorn tree in the yard and listening to the cranes at the city dump two blocks away scoop up crushed aluminum, that if I could record "this": parents fighting, squirrels crunching acorns, garbage sorted like bad memories, that if I could find words to make sense of my own life, I could write anything. But in the neighborhood I grew up in, to be a writer meant to be a dead English novelist, like Charles Dickens. It simply wasn't done. Some people had heard of Ernest Hemingway, but you had to know something about fishing and bull fighting. Women writers usually went mad or changed their names to George. I wanted to continue to be a female person, and I wanted to tell "the truth." I wanted to explore "real life." Mine, at least for starters. I would have liked to have written my memoirs, but only famous people wrote their memoirs. To my teachers, writing about "real life" meant only one thing, and I was tracked early on to write for newspapers.

By the time I got to high school I was writing most of the feature stories on our school paper. I was often asked to go after "difficult and sensitive" subjects that required intimate self-disclosures from the interviewees. My portfolio is filled with family tales of woe and grief. Picture me at fifteen, asking a laid-off worker from the Acorn Chemical Corporation plant, the father of eight, what it feels like now that his house has just burned down and all of his family's possessions have been destroyed. Imagine me interviewing the pastor's wife after her son, who was in my homeroom on the rare days he showed up, has just fatally overdosed on windowpane. It is no wonder that I was soon nicknamed The Sob Story Queen.

I did not know that I would someday decide I had exploited the people I wrote about. It never occurred to me to question why these stories did not satisfy my burning desire to write, or why, after writing them quickly and easily, I would hop on the back of Gary Pritchik's big black motorcycle and ride to the river where we tried again and again, beneath the blinking yellow factory lights, to set the Cuyahoga on fire. As a highschooler, I did not aim to achieve High Art; I wanted to pile up enough extracurricular activities on my record to get into a decent college as far away from Cleveland as possible.

When I was asked to write a feature story on a friend of mine named Sharon who was suffering from lupus, I realized that I was getting uncomfortable with this form of writing. I did it anyway, and the story won me a major journalism prize in Ohio, plus a scholarship to the Medill School of Journalism at Northwestern University, but it cost me a friend. After I wrote the story, Sharon and I simply never felt comfortable with one another again. It was as though, as Native Americans once said about their photographers, that I had stolen her soul. What interests me now about this incident is that out of all the people who might have written the article, I was truly the most familiar with Sharon's Before and After Story, because I knew her body like I knew my own.

Sharon and I had gone on our first diet together in eighth grade. We had taken each other's measurements week after week and finally, one spring morning, had pronounced each other beautiful. We had coached each other on what to expect from boys. None of that was in the story because my hard-nosed editor would have written "who cares?" across the front with his favorite grease pencil. Sharon remained an Other and her situation was simply tragic. Stripped of the noisy, meddling "I," the writer whose observations affect and interact with and ultimately bring life to the observed, Sharon as subject was now reduced to an object; she was not that living, wisecracking teenage girl with whom I'd once compared bellies and thighs.

Our first year in journalism school we had to take a course called Basic Writing; 50% of our grade was based on our final feature story, which would be read in front of the class. I had not written a feature since the one I wrote on Sharon, and I was gun-shy. I searched the campus desperately for story ideas until one day, in the middle of Sex Role Socialization Class, my professor told us about a fascinating woman she'd met at a party the night before who was a pre-school teacher by day, and madam for the most elite massage parlor in Chicago by night. This was before the time when we began to have suspicions about some of our pre-school teachers. The madam—whose name I've since forgotten but it was something very unexotic, like Doris—would be coming to the next class, and was eager to talk to any of us in private.

The next Saturday the madam drove out to Evanston in her beat-up orange Opal and sat across from me in my dorm room beneath my Arthur Rackham poster of Alice in Wonderland, eating the cookies and milk I'd bought at the campus snackshop. She reminded me of Mama Cass turned bombshell in her flowing Indian skirts and her low-cut blouse with the shiny red heart she'd lipsticked on her considerable cleavage. When she laughed her whole body shook, and the heart bobbed up and down like a fish. Outside the window there were kids playing frisbee while she told me everything I wanted to know, and more. Finally, after we'd talked for hours, she picked up my stuffed koala bear with its N.U. garter belt looped around its waist like a goofy satin hoola hoop, and she set it down again on top of the tape recorder. "You aren't going to get the real story inside your sweet little ivory tower over here," she said. "If you really want to know your material, you have to spend a day at 'the house.'"

"The house" was not as seedy as I'd imagined. The "waiting area" was furnished discreetly with beige couches and chairs, Impressionist prints, potted plants, and a stereo that was playing the Brandenburg Concertos. I would have thought I was in an upscale dentist's office if not for the two women posing at the window in fancy lingerie. One of these women told me that before she'd started hooking six months before she'd only slept with one man in her life, her abusive ex-husband. She was 27. She looked at me with anger, imagining condemnation in my eyes. The other woman was 18, just my age, and I took to her immediately. Both were black, although the madam assured me that the massage parlor was a veritable melting pot of colors and Chicago neighborhoods, and that white girls who looked like junior varsity cheerleaders were in high demand.

As the madam had promised, the house catered to men's fantasies, and women were hired on the basis of whether or not they fit a "type." There was also a room full of costumes and make-up, which could have serviced a theater's full repertory season, from *Macbeth* to *A Streetcar Named Desire*. My new friend, the 18-year-old, was six feet tall, and she'd been hired to deal specifically with men who needed women to be big. Her most frequent client was a prosecuting attorney who happened to be nearly seven feet tall. When he appeared socially with his wife, who was not quite five feet, people called them Mutt and Jeff. When the prosecutor visited the house, his lady for hire donned boxing gloves, duked it out with him in their imaginary ring, and knocked him down. Afterwards he would leap up unharmed, take off his gloves and hers, measure all 72 inches of her against the bedroom door with a yardstick, and then promptly carry her to bed, a redeemed slugger.

Then there was the pediatric prof at the medical school who wrote medical books by day and kinky fairy tales at night. The management required its women to be 18-and-over but they had no trouble finding voting age gals who *looked* undeveloped, ponytailed, and girly-girlish enough to play Little Red Riding Hood to his Big Bad Wolf in those alliterative scripts he brought with him. And then there was the tax accountant necrophiliac.

The only client I talked to was the priest, who went there every Sunday after church and stayed all day. He loved to bake for his women and today he brought a loaf of bread that we all broke together and washed down with Diet Pepsi instead of wine. He was a lonely, inarticulate man with a voice that sighed instead of sang, and I could not imagine him inspiring fervor and faith from behind his pulpit. Nor, for that matter, could I—or did I want to—picture him naked and panting with one of these women, but that's exactly what I ultimately saw. Just as I was getting ready to leave, the 27-year-old insisted that if I were a true journalist and not a princess from the suburbs that I'd complete my research from behind the bedroom door. Before I could think about it I was in the same room with them, watching, notebook in hand, while they oiled, massaged, and stroked the priest to transcendence, all "on the house."

That night, tucked safely inside my dorm room, I began to wade through all this rich material. Immediately I was pressed with many writerly problems. How was I to deal with point of view? Whose story was it? The working women's? The clients'? My original goal had been to profile the madam, but she was swiftly being eclipsed by the prosecutor, the pediatrician, the necrophiliac, and the priest, who were all far stranger than she was. How much of the dirt should I put in? What should I leave to the imagination? What about what I'd seen with my own eyes inside that room?

I finally chose to make the place and its strange characters the subject of my article, and to do this I took myself entirely out of the story. I wrote it as though I were a bug on the wall watching a typical day in the house, but I tried to use the voice of the madam as much as I could.

As it turned out, the t.a. took me aside later and told me he thought I could publish it in *The Chicago Reader*. Other students in the class had interviewed the Chicago journalists they hoped to line up internships with for the summer and he and the prof were thankful that I'd gone for something with "grit." There was only one problem, he said, and that was the style. It was simply too literary. If I cut out all the adjectives, he said, I would be on my way to becoming a journalist.

I turned down his generous offer, as flattered as I was, because I'd promised the women I wouldn't publish the piece. Now that I look back, it seems that there were other reasons why I didn't want to sell this story to the *Reader*. One was that I wasn't interested in developing the dry, "just the facts" style that the t.a. thought I needed to master in order to become a valid journalist. The other reason was that the real story for me was not, as everyone supposed, that respectable professional men can be sleazy but simply that an 18-year-old girl/woman with Arthur Rackham posters and a stuffed koala bear with a Northwestern garter belt had been in this place and talked to these people and seen what she'd seen, and that she had somehow been changed by having told this story. My problem, in 1976, was that I didn't know of a journalistic form that would allow me to tell it the way it wanted to be told; those new literary journalists were not yet being taught. But neither, I discovered when I switched into creative writing, could it be told in a poem or short story.

Poetry writing was a two-quarter sequence taught by a woman who was writing her doctoral dissertation on the Modernist poets. Each week she had us read several volumes of the poet of the week—Eliot, Pound, Moore, Bogan, Stevens, Williams, and others—and then write two poems, the first a "pastiche" for which we obviously stole not only the poet's technical bag of tricks but his or her material as well, and the other an "imitation" for which we borrowed a technique but still tried to write our own poem. By the end of the first semester, whatever "voice" we'd all had before had been consumed by the tones and postures of our Modernist mentors. We would call each other on the phone and say, "How do you write a poem?"

The summer after that workshop I went to Wesleyan College and attended my first writers' conference. My workshop teacher read my poems and was kind enough to point out the origins of each line in my work. "That's from Shakespeare's Sonnet 18," he said, "and that's from 'The Love Song of J. Alfred Prufrock,' " and "that's one of Louise Bogan's metaphors for depression. Where are you in these poems?"

A year or so later I went to one of my old poetry teacher's readings. She closed with a poem about the town where she'd grown up, which was somewhere — I couldn't believe it — in the South. I'd always assumed, given her diction, that she'd spent much of her life in English boarding schools. Maybe she had. Then it dawned on me. On a certain level, my teacher's aspirations to literary academia may have been spawned by a profound self-hatred. As mine had. Along with the dreams of countless other girl-women I knew skulking around miserably in the library. If my teacher had exerted so much energy trying to transform herself from the down home girl to the Oxford poet scholar, then how could she help me go deep into myself to find my authentic voice and material and story? I signed up for fiction writing and hoped for the best.

The fiction writing class was taught by a tall, trim, blue-jeaned, very hip late-thirtyish fellow who was nicknamed "The Marlboro Man" by the circle of female students who had crushes on him. He had a slight Western twang and wore cowboy boots. When he came to our parties he smoked pot with us and told humorous anecdotes about the famous writers he'd met. His class was entertaining and lively. We got to write about subjects closer to our own lives, but there was still a lot of stigma against being "self-indulgent" and "autobiographical." Style was more important than content — you had to be slick and exude a certain daring razzmatazz. You couldn't be political or direct. Processing personal experience was only okay if you applied heavy irony. Think of the times. It was now 1978, and people everywhere were trying to numb their pain from the previous decade by wearing shiny half-buttoned shirts and jumping into vats of hot water with near-strangers to the beat of the Bee Gees.

Although there was some lip service paid to original "voice" and "place" in my writing training, the fashionable voices were usually male back then: Bellow, Nabokov, Gass, excerpts from Pyncheon, and a smattering of Ishmael Reed for color. I felt pressure to rev up my narrative engine, just as, when the Carver school made the grade soon thereafter, I felt pressure to edit everything back out except for the name brand products. And as far as place was concerned, it seemed to me you had only two choices. You could write about rural New England, of course, or you could write about the gritty "mean streets" of a Chicago, L.A., or New York. But what about a place as modest and chintzy as Cleveland, nicknamed The Mistake by the Lake? When I looked out the window I saw not Mt. Monadnock, not the pushers at the subway, but a few scrappy trees and a mechanical crane devouring crushed cars. I wrote stories, back then, set in places I'd never been, like Paris and Barcelona and San Francisco, because, it seemed, my own eyes had never seen anything worth mentioning.

I've heard that when Annie Dillard first began writing what became *Pilgrim at Tinker Creek*, she intended to set it in Acadia National Park in Maine and write it in third person, in the voice of a *50-year-old male academic metaphysician*. After a time she realized that she didn't know Acadia the way she knew her home in Virginia, but it took a great deal of coaxing on the part of an enlightened editor to get her to write it in her own young female voice. This book, published just a year before I started college, points to a problem that women and people of color have always had in this country. Many of us have gotten one too many "who cares?" written in red ink on our work. I think it is very common for the writer, especially the student writer, to approach a writing project with the feeling I am not worthy, as I am, with what I know now, to tell this story as I see it in my own words. To be an authority on this subject I have to hide behind the voice of someone else, perhaps someone whiter, with more Y chromosomes; to sound like I've "been around" I have to be from New York, or London, or Paris, or a charming old farm in New England with a ghost in the apple orchard who recites Robert Frost.

It was not until I was nearly 30—just as memoir and the whole genre of creative nonfiction began to flower—that the stories from my life I'd tried to disguise and romanticize in fiction came exploding, honestly and urgently, onto the page. As a writer, a teacher, and a reader myself, I have come to see that today's readers are hungering for I-as-eye-witness truth, perhaps because we live in an age where it is now commonly known that our political leaders are liars and thieves. People are choosing to learn about Vietnamese war brides, the years of Stalin, and the American 1950s not from the so-called expert historians or the ruling patriarchs who led from inside their offices, but from "real people" whose solitary landscapes and single voices have a power that illuminates the larger humanity we all share—which makes, as the short story once did, the strange familiar and the familiar strange.

Just as readers are hungry to learn the truth in a language that is more lively than they find in the daily papers, our students yearn to tell their own truths and to come to understand themselves and their connection to the world better in the process. Creative nonfiction is a genre in which student writers can use their authentic voices and make no bones about their presence in the work. They can write about places they know well. They can feel that what they have seen with their own eyes is of literary value, and of human value to others.

It is my belief that education should be a nourishing place for the heart and soul as well as the mind, and it should build confidence, not destroy it. How do we help our students draw on their own resources, not just their acquired knowledge? The teaching of creative nonfiction can validate the students' current lives, and strengthen their writing skills. Nonfiction writing in first person teaches the young writer to sharpen her powers of observation and use of memory, to hone his specificity and finesse for naming concrete things, and to create an honest, living voice. For the student writer, the permission to write about something he or she passionately cares about is what motivates that writer to go the extra mile to make the prose vivid and clear, rather than flat, empty, and vague. To write first-person nonfiction well, one must make contact with what Brenda Ueland calls "our True Self, the very Center, for ... here lies all originality, talent, honor, truthfulness, courage and cheerfulness."

I suspect that had courses in creative nonfiction been available to me back in Cleveland, I could have saved myself about 15 years' worth of writing mistakes.

Perhaps one day when encouraging a student to seek her

"True Self" in nonfiction prose is a basic component of writing pedagogy and not some retrograde Sixties concept, it will be customary to write "Why do *you* care about this?" on student essays, instead of "who cares?" Perhaps helping our students search for "the very Center" right from the start will save them several years of writing mistakes. Whereas William Gass, in his introduction to *In the Heart of the Heart of Country*, advises the aspiring young fiction writer always to "wait five years," the young nonfiction writer who has found his or her voice can often master a particular piece of memoir well enough to create something worthwhile and even publishable right now.

WILLIAM KITTREDGE

DEATH OF THE WESTERN

CULTUREFRONT

Driving south across Nevada on Highway 95, through the steely afternoon distances, you get the sense that you are in a country where nobody will cut you any slack at all. You are in a version of the American West where you are on your own; the local motto is take care of your own damned self. That's where I was, just south to Tonapah, maybe 150 miles north of Las Vegas, dialing across the radio, when I heard the news that Louis L'Amour was dead of lung cancer at the age of 80.

They said he had published 101 books. The first was *Hondo*, in 1953, which was made into a movie starring John Wayne. It seemed right. The way I saw L'Amour, in the eye of my mind, he even looked like John Wayne. Remember that old man, perishing of cancer in *The Shootist*?

If you had never lived in the American West, you might have felt elegiac, and you imagined the last of the old legendary Westerners were dying. I knew better. I grew up on a horseback cattle ranch and I knew a lot of those old hard-eyed bastards. They're not dying out. What was passing was another round of make-believe.

The old true Westerners I knew never had the time of day for shootout movies, and they mostly thought western novels were just so much nonsense. They would soon tell you that much of what passes as authenticity in the Western, no matter how colorful and indigenous it might seem, was all about ten percent wrong and must have come from library research. I remember my grandfather's scorn for a pulp paper copy of *Ranch Romances* he found in the bunkhouse when I was a kid. "Book people," my grandfather said. "Nobody ever lived like that."

Driving Nevada, I felt a kind of two-hearted sadness over the death of Louis L'Amour. He so clearly loved the West and the dreams of the good strong people he found there, and yet he so deeply transmogrified any sense of the real life there that my grandfather might have understood and respected.

Most of us understand that the West we find in a Louis L'Amour novel didn't really exist much of anywhere. A lot of any art is trumped-up. We excuse it. Out in the Armagosa Valley of southern Nevada, just west of where I was traveling on Highway 95, there are great dunes of yellow sand that have stood in for Africa and Arabia through all the history of movies. You don't hear much complaining about that kind of artifice.

There's a darker problem with the Western. It's a story inhabited by a mythology about power and the social utility of violence, an American version of an ancient dream of warrior righteousness. Because of that, it's a story many of us find threatening. We don't want to live in a society fascinated by fantasies of killer wish-fulfillment. We keep hoping the Western will just go away. But it won't. From *The Song of Roland* to *Shane* to *Star Wars*, these hero stories just duck out of sight, like Clark Kent stepping into a telephone booth, and re-emerge with renewed vitality.

The dreaming goes on. We all know how Westerns proceed. There is the society of good simple folk who only want to live decent lives, and there are the evil unshaven bad guys, driven by undisciplined lusts and greed. And there is the hero, who cuts through the shit. Shane straps on his sixguns and solves the problem of Jack Palance. The obvious implications, taken seriously by a society like ours, so deeply and often frustrated, and so adept in the sciences of destruction, are literally unthinkable. Nuke the bastards.

After the Lone Ranger we get Dirty Harry and Rambo. In times many of us understand as awash in moral disorder, mostly because our problems are so complex as to defy clean quick-fix solutions, we yearn for simplicities, and it's natural enough some of us might dream of escaping into an imagined gunfighter past, and yearn to clear the decks. Enough with ambiguities.

So, when people told me the death of Louis L'Amour meant we were finally done with such stories, I had to say I didn't think so. At all. Louis L'Amour wrote books about a world in which moral problems were clearly defined, and strong men stepped forward to solve them. Millions of people seem to have found it a very comfortable dream to inhabit. The old hero story, in some form, is going to be with us a long time. And there's nothing so terrible about that; it's just that we have to keep from forgetting it's a fantasy and always was.

The thing I most strongly dislike about the Western is personal, and has much to do with my love of the kind of country where I had always lived. What I resent is the way the Western has deluded so many of us in the West for so long.

The Western told us that we were living the right lives, and that we would be rewarded if only we would persevere. That message was a clear simple-minded lie. Driving Nevada, thinking about the death of Louis L'Amour and the shells of burnt-out hotels in one-time mining towns like Goldfield and Rhyolite, I felt anger ringing in me like the empty buzzing of locusts.

The dim shadows of leafy poplar far off against the mountains, with Death Valley beyond, were sure signs of pump agriculture. Right over there people were exhausting aquifers, which had taken millennia to accumulate. And what energy there was in the little roadside clusterings of bars and cafés and brothels that comprise towns like Lathrop Wells and Indian Springs, along the highway on the western fringe of the Nuclear Testing Site, seemed painted on.

That roadside West is like a shabby imitation of our cowboy dreams, a sad compromised place, used and abused, and used again. So many of the people there feel deceived, and with good reason. They believed in promises implicit in the Western, that they had a right to a good life in this place, and it has become clear to them that it was all a major lie. *Take care of your own damned self.* Nobody is bullet-proof.

What we need in our West is another kind of story, in which we can see ourselves for what we mostly are, decent people striving to form and continually reform a just society in which we can find some continuity, taking care in the midst of the useful and significant lives. We're finding such storytelling, slowly, in books like *Housekeeping* and *A River Runs Through It*, in the stories and essays and novels of writers like Mary Clearman Blew and Terry Tempest Williams and James Welch and Ivan Doig, Cormac McCarthy and Louise Erdrich and Leslie Silko and James Galvin, and so many others. It's part of my two-hearted sadness that Louis L'Amour couldn't have come to appreciate the flowering of a genuine literature in the West he so loved.

EDWARD ALBEE

ON PLAYWRITING

DRAMATICS

There are a couple of things you should know. I am a playwright. I've written twenty-six plays, I think, in the past thirty-three years, which makes me a little less lazy than I sometimes think I am. Some of them have been very popular, which means people have come to see them. Some have been very unpopular.

Sometimes, being a little protective of the least popular, sometimes I think the least popular ones are superior to the more popular ones. One of the things you learn very quickly in our society is that there is not necessarily much relationship between popularity and excellence. Quite often the very best stuff is participated in by the fewest people. But you mustn't fall into the trap, either, of assuming that because nobody likes what you have done it is very good. Sometimes people don't like what you've done because it is terrible. We'll talk about that possibility, too.

It is a tough racket. It can be pretty heartbreaking, and you really have to, deep down, have a toughness to yourself, or you're not going to be able to survive in the theatre.

ON WHERE THE IDEAS FOR PLAYS COME FROM

Damned if I know. All of a sudden one day I'll be going about my own business, walking around or something, and I'll suddenly realize that I must have been thinking about a play for quite a while, even though I didn't know I was thinking about it.

Because by the time I become aware that I have been thinking about a play, it's coming along quite nicely. The characters are there, the situation has begun to create itself.

I'm sure the creativity, where the ideas come from, comes from the unconscious part of the mind, which as you know makes up 90 percent of the mind. I'm convinced that is where the ideas originate, they evolve and eventually enter into the conscious mind. You keep working on them, and then eventually you write them down.

ON HIS METHOD OF WORKING

When I sit down I don't know what the first line of the play is going to be. I know what the destination is, but I don't have any idea necessarily how I am going to get there. I believe in letting the characters determine that in their situation. How they behave determines where it goes.

I try to stand back and sort of push them and guide them so the thing won't go off in all sorts of directions that it shouldn't go off in. I believe that when the characters do that it's really me doing that, since the characters can't do anything unless I tell them what to do. They don't exist. They really do exist, but they don't. They can't say anything unless I write it down for them. It is a trick you play on yourself, thinking that the characters are doing your work when really you're doing it and assigning it to the various characters.

I'm not one of these playwrights — and I'm not saying you shouldn't be this kind of playwright — I'm not one of these playwrights who writes a twenty-five-page synopsis of what the play is going to be about. I don't write down histories of the natures of the characters. I don't plot out each scene before I write it.

The only thing I do is when it is ready, when it is time to start writing something down, I wait longer than most playwrights do. Sometimes I keep an idea in my head five or six years before I'll write it down. I start at the beginning and write straight through to the end. That's the way I write. It's nice that way. You have lots of surprises. You discover all sorts of things that you were planning to do that you didn't know you were going to do.

ON THE IDEAL CONDITIONS FOR WRITING

I think it is probably better to be awake, sober, and drug-free. I suspect those three conditions are probably helpful. But beyond that, I just have to feel like writing. I'm not one of these people who goes to the desk every single day and writes. I wait until my head gets filled with stuff and I have to get it out of my head.

I used to drink occasionally and take a little grass now and again back when I was real young. And I thought that I could write an awful lot better if I did. But it wasn't very good. It seemed wonderful at the time. Marvelous. I'd look at it the next day and say, "What the hell was that all about?"

ON THE IMPORTANCE OF CONFLICT IN DRAMA

Plays are basically about something that is wrong. Plays are about people that are not getting along with each other terribly well. Situations that are wrong. Most serious plays, good plays, are about something that's wrong that should be corrected. You can't write a very good play about a bunch of people getting along with each other very, very well and there is absolutely no argument. You can't do it. It's not going to be a play. There has to be conflict. And until the conflict is resolved there is tension, because of the conflict. People in conflict with each other, people in conflict with society, their government, philosophically, politically, socially. There is conflict and conflict produces tension. And the solution to the problem releases tension and that is probably when the play should end.

ON A PLAYWRIGHT'S SOURCES OF THE DETAILS OF CHARACTER

You keep your eyes and ears open and store it away until you need it. Part of it comes from yourself. You can't write a character unless you can get inside the character and imagine the way the character thinks.

And the rest you make up. You invent. That's why you're able to write men, women, young people, old people, black, white, no matter who or what you are. It's your responsibility and your ability to be able to do all that. You have to be able to put yourself into whatever character you are writing. So you look and listen and make things up.

ON STUDYING THE WORK OF OTHER PLAYWRIGHTS

There are some twentieth century playwrights that I think it is very important for anybody who wants to be a playwright to know about. You start with Chekhov, one of the first great playwrights of the twentieth century. Then you have Pirandello, an extraordinary playwright that not enough people know about. And there is Brecht, a real interesting playwright, and Samuel Beckett, who may be the best of the bunch. He and Chekhov may be the best of the bunch. You have those four. That's a pretty good group to study.

But let me tell you one thing, if you are going to learn from other writers, don't only read the great ones, because if you do that you'll get so filled with despair and the fear that you'll never be able to do anywhere near as well as they did that you'll stop writing. I recommend that you read a lot of bad stuff, too. It's very encouraging. "Hey, I can do so much better than this." Read the greatest stuff but read the stuff that isn't so great, too. Great stuff is very discouraging. If you read only Beckett and Chekhov you'll go away and only deliver telegrams at Western Union.

ON BEING TRUE TO ONE'S OWN VISION

They tell you that commercial plays should be little over two hours long. A play should be as long as it needs to be. It can be ten minutes, it can be seven hours. What should the play be about? It should be about whatever you can make a stage experience, only that. Whatever you can make valid. What style should it be written it? Whatever style is right for the play.

There are no limits, you see, except succeeding at what you do. In the commercial theatre they want certain things. They want happy problems. They want the plays to be a certain length. They want everybody to be able to walk out of the theatre fairly happy. If it can be a musical, so much the better. That's what the commercial theatre is all about. If you're that kind of a writer, okay. But if you're the kind of writer who wants to write a very grim, seven-hour play, then that's what you should write. If you want to write a play so angry, so filled with rage, that it practically takes the audience and hits them in the head or slaps them in the face, then that's the kind of play you should write.

You should write exactly what the play needs to be and pay no attention to anything else. That's all that matters. The rest is commerce, the rest is compromise. You'll be asked to do a lot of that, but hold off. One of the lovely things about being a playwright is that you can do whatever you want to do. While a lot of people would rather you do something else, they can't stop you.

ON COLLABORATION

Now, if you're in rehearsal for the first time with your play and the director says to you, maybe that scene is a little long, you may want to think about cutting it. Pay a little attention; maybe the director is right.

You go back and you look at the scene and say yes, that scene seems long. Then you have to say to yourself, does this scene seem long because I wrote it too long or because of the way it is being directed? If the director directed it differently would it still seem too long? So maybe you will ask that the scene be directed differently.

If you realize the scene is too long no matter how it is directed, then you realize, gee, I wrote this scene too long, maybe I better cut it a little bit. Then you make your own cuts. You have to be very careful because sometimes suggestions are not made to help the play but to help actors or to make things easier. You have the right to not change anything, but don't be a fool. Change things if somebody else is right.

But if you do change something because somebody else is right, you must instantly take credit for it yourself. That's very important.

EDNA O'BRIEN

IT'S A BAD TIME OUT THERE FOR EMOTION

THE NEW YORK TIMES BOOK REVIEW

Each of us looks for something different in a work of fiction. Some like the ordinary so as to feel reaffirmed and "at home," and some seek the extraordinary, those daring distortions of realism that, by stunning verbal feats, hurtle the reader to fantastic latitudes. There is, however, just that element of strain when the conscious and not the unconscious is seen to be pulling the strings. Magic, as I see it, is simple eeriness, as in, say, "The Snow Queen," when Gerda asks the forest raven where her friend has gone and he replies, "I'll tell you . . . but if only you understood raven speech I could tell you better"; or in the enchanted stories of Isaac Bashevis Singer, in which New York is often fleetingly transformed into an exile's dreamland; or in Kafka's work, in which the ordinary glides inexorably into the gilded labyrinths of nightmare.

Some read to laugh, and let it be hoped some still read to cry, so that on finishing "Bleak House" they realize more fully than from any formal education the perversity, torpidity and mindless callousness of humankind. Some choose to enter the dark chambers of the psyche and reread Dostoyevsky, not so much to feel at home as to become guests to the criminal within themselves. Some like to sample the nausea of life, man's fate reduced to the absurd by writers who curse God, like Samuel Beckett. That author once put it to me that my return to my native land, both in fiction and in person, was to imbibe another dose of disgust. I could not agree, no more than I would agree that absurdity is

Beckett's prime agenda. Rather, I would say it is a hectic delirium that inclines toward the profane but always ends on a note of liturgical grace.

Some look for more than one thing, and others like me look for everything. Reading "The Island" by Gustaw Herling of late, I felt an exhilaration that was like the exhilaration of that first moment of being touched and in some way shattered by great prose. I do not remember what that prose was, whether it was Joyce or Chekhov, but it was one or the other because my reading material was scant.

At that time I owned two books — "The Steppe," by Chekhov, and "Introducing James Joyce," by T.S. Eliot. In those days I tended to identify with the young boy in "The Steppe," separated from his mother and baffled by the grown-ups he was traveling with; but now boy, grown-ups and landscape all have their piercing effect, their fates joined inextricably, like the threads of a tapestry. Likewise with Joyce. I was at that time drawn to the chapter in "A Portrait of the Artist as a Young Man" describing the festive Christmas dinner and the (not unusual) Irish eruption when sex-cum-politics, in the person of Parnell, is raised and enmity let loose. Nowadays the "moon gray" wanderings of Anna Livia Plurabelle make my blood run cold. One rereading of a book digs the trench for the next and the next.

Rereading "The Steppe," in its beautiful Everyman edition, I realized that what Chekhov does above all else is address the spiritual gnaw within the reader, and this is a consideration lamentably absent from most fiction today. Indeed, so does Joyce. That Jesuit-denouncing ventriloquist was as religious as they come, not with the religion of dogma or faith but of transubstantiation through words. While depicting the locale so precisely, or the hop of a kidney on a frying pan, he constantly and by a weird escalation of thought transfigures things so that a Paris street "rawly waking" *is* a Paris street and also one that no mortal will ever tread. He is realist, magic realist and spiritual genie — Father, Son and Holy Ghost.

So what I want most in fiction is the spiritual thrust, the moment or sequence of moments that shifts the boundaries to something larger, familiar and also startling, to the brush with God and nature or the absence of God and nature. Is this the result of a Catholic upbringing, the sensibility inherited from a race steeped in suffering? No. Every nation has suffered, yet her writers deal differently with that legacy. Brecht gave us a lasting heroine in Mother Courage, a creature who would sacrifice almost anything for cash, and while I admire her worldly pluck I would not make the journey with her frequently. There is a spiritual vacancy, a pragmatism, an absence of psychic shudder.

The Russians, the Poles and the Irish — or, to be precise, some Russians, Poles and Irish — seem to be the least ashamed of and the most atavistic at mapping out a landscape of suffering. In Gustaw Herling's tales, for instance, the gravedigger is never absent from the carnival, and fatality presides like a lodestar. Some might call this masochism, but they would be mistaken. Joyce himself said that one has not lived unless one has conceived of life as a tragedy. Yet his prose has a fierce ebullience, and here we must make the distinction between what tragedy exacts and depression produces, depression spawning an industry of literary knitting.

When Chekhov, that most dissecting of writers, decides to devote 183 pages in "The Duel" to the history of a discontented man whose wife is dying, whose children are neglected and whose sexual urges cannot be met, it is not simply a little tale of infidelity; it is the gouging of the human heart, the moral prig as well as the moral dodger in us all, the insatiability of human nature and the little graph of each private fall.

There is a notion nowadays, meretricious as most notions are, that to write of such things is secondary and holds no brief in these apocalyptic times, when war, rape, murder and carnage fill our television screens and our newspapers and haunt our everyday lives to the extent that we send a donation or have a gruesome twist to our nightmares. The fact that one theme should cancel out the other is buncombe.

Loneliness, physical and metaphysical, is stamped on every face I see and surely not appeased by most film and television fare, with its kindergarten psychology, cretinous language and flurry of bullets flying about with the ennui of confetti. Chekhov or any other true artist would indeed write about the war, the rape, the carnage, were he part of it, as for instance Curzio Malaparte so convincingly did in "The Skin," but the imperative must come from within. The inside is where everything, including the first murmur of language, gestates and waits to be born. Sometimes it waits forever.

Let me say that I think the excellence, rigorousness and lucidity of serious journalism surpasses most published fiction. But information is not transcendence and fact not always the touchstone of feeling. We hear a great deal (too much) about politically correct or incorrect material, but we hear nothing when that judgment is transferred to feeling. It has been sent underground, but like one of Kafka's animals it scrapes its way up so that we come upon the work of Gustaw Herling or his fellow Pole Zbigniew Herbert, both of whom, despite untold obstacles, deliver psalms of passion and luminousness.

In the Rainer Werner Fassbinder movie "The Marriage of Maria Braun," Maria tells a man in prison that it is a bad time out in the world for emotion. Why is this? When was it pronounced taboo? Who is to blame? Is it the overweening influence of the chic or a mix of the chic with the serious or the single-line mantra repetition of pop songs, in which sense is subsumed by sound? It is these things and many more, but I also think it is the prevailing ethos of literary criticism, which, especially in England, inclines to the scalping, where the clever bow to the clever, where the merest manifestation of feeling is pilloried and where consideration of language itself is zero. An indication of a country whose horizons have narrowed and with them any visionary or cultural largess. This is more insidious than it might seem. It breaks faith with innocence, refutes the collective imagination and inculcates a literary climate of smugness and provincialism. Within it lies the sick kernel of inferiority that leads only to yobbery.

The point of literature is not or should not be a question of scoring. Faulkner does not vanquish Hemingway. Recently reading novels by those two robust and linguistic dazzlers Denis Johnson and Cormac McCarthy, I could not favor "Jesus' Son" above "All the Pretty Horses." And neither diminished the pleasure of reading "The Crystal Desert," by David G. Campbell, a nonfiction work of flawless prose, in which the plants, rocks and glaciers of Antarctica are treated with the same particularity as the characters in a novel. All three are a feast.

Literary prizes are another bogy if you think that because Joyce never won the Nobel Prize whereas Yeats did, Yeats was a more important writer. They are indeed different in their sublimity, though I would argue that Joyce stands as the master builder of Irish writing and English writing in this century—a droll aside on the vengeance that history wreaks. Like other truly great writers, Joyce was offhand, albeit totally confident, about his work, and he concluded that the money spent on a copy of "Ulysses" might provide about the same satisfaction as that spent on a pound of chops.

Chops or not, literature is the last banquet between minds. It is true, as Romain Rolland said, that literature is useless against reality while being a great consolation to the individual. But it is increasingly clear that the fate of the universe will come to depend more and more on individuals as the bungling of bureaucracy permeates every corner of our existence.

Books are the Grail for what is deepest, more mysterious and least expressible within ourselves. They are our soul's skeleton. If we were to forget that, it would prefigure how false and feelingless we could become.

MILLER WILLIAMS

THE WRITING OF "ADJUSTING TO THE LIGHT" AND "AN AUGUST EVENING OUTSIDE OF NASHVILLE"

WRITER'S DIGEST

I don't like poems that seem to say, "Guess what I mean." And I don't much like symbolist poems, in which people and things are standing in for the real subjects, who for some reason are absent. I also don't care for surreal or impressionist poems that assume a reader wants to help interpret the poet's dreams.

This is not to say that I think everything in a poem should be on the surface. Not at all. It's simply to say that there should *be* a surface, a place for the reader to stand. Young journalists used to be taught to answer the questions *who, what, where, when* and *why* in the first compressed paragraph of a story. I would go so far as to say that the first four of these ought to be answered in a single reading of most poems.

But this is only a starting place. Because the question to ask is not, finally, "What does a poem mean?" but "How does a poem mean?" as John Ciardi and I tried to make clear in our textbook by that name.

Look from this perspective at the poem on the next page, "Adjusting to the Light."

The dramatic situation is clear enough. Lazarus has just been revived. He speaks, and then his sisters speak. He is understandably confused. He is told—though he may not be paying a lot of attention—that his return from the dead is going to call for a lot of adjustment on the part of several people, including Lazarus himself.

ADJUSTING TO THE LIGHT

—air—air! I can barely breathe . . . aah!
Whatever it was, I think I shook it off.
Except my head hurts and I stink. Except
what is this place and what am I doing here?

Brother, you're in a tomb. You were dead four days.
Jesus came and made you alive again.

Lazarus, listen, we have things to tell you.
We killed the sheep you meant to take to market.
We couldn't keep the old dog, either.
He minded you. The rest of us he barked at.
Rebecca, who cried two days, has given her hand
to the sandalmaker's son. Please understand
we didn't know that Jesus could do this.

We're glad you're back. But give us time to think.
Imagine our surprise to have you—well,
not well, but weller. I'm sorry, but you do stink.
Everyone, give us some air. We want to say
we're sorry for all of that. And one thing more.
We threw away the lyre. But listen, we'll pay
whatever the sheep was worth. The dog, too.
And put your room the way it was before.

But it would be wrong, in a sense, to say that the poem is
"about" Lazarus. A young woman recently noted in an interview
with me that she could see in my poetry influences of my father,
who was a Methodist minister. When I asked for an example, she
referred to this poem, "the one," she said, "about resurrection."

"That poem," I said, "is only incidentally about resurrection.
At heart, it's about questioning. It questions the simplicity of the
story as we have it in the Bible, and the happy consequence of
miracles."

Nearly every poem, at heart, is a questioning, a way of saying, "We don't have the whole story," or "We may not have been looking at this thing in the right light," or "Let's just check behind this curtain to see if there's somebody else in the room."

Browning's "My Last Duchess," Eliot's "The Love Song of J. Alfred Prufrock," Bishop's "The Fish"—each is a way of questioning what we have thought.

In its own small way, so is "Adjusting to the Light" a questioning. So what does it mean? It means that the stories we hear and tell are more complicated than we usually allow, because people's lives and deaths are more tangled up in one another than we want to realize.

How the poem means calls attention to a number of other matters.

It means—that is, it works—by inviting the reader inside to take part in the making of the poem, as all poems must. This is done by an appeal to the reader's sense, imagination, emotion and intellect. Before I go further, I ought to share something of the way in which I write and some of the assumptions about the nature of poetry out of which I write.

I don't write in measured feet, but in counted stresses, as there are five stresses to the line in "Adjusting to the Light." Very frequently I write not in a rhyme pattern, but with scattered rhyme. Both elements of style lend themselves to the conversational quality that I'm comfortable with in my poetry. But I may cast a poem in regular rhyme if I want to be less conversational, as I did here with "An August Evening Outside of Nashville."

AN AUGUST EVENING
OUTSIDE OF NASHVILLE

Seeing a chipmunk in the yard
holding a nut between its paws
while a jay in cold regard,
in a kind of punk repose,
sheds upon it what might be
contempt, for birds in Tennessee;

Following a changing cloud
while my eyelids fill with lead;
hearing the wild bees grow loud
while a wobbling, overfed
goose scolds a lazy dog
and fungus on a rotting log

makes shapes I find a message in;
when a breeze takes the sweat
barely off my bare skin,
I can almost forget
how you were with dirty feet
all tangled in my sweaty sheet.

Everything a poet does in a poem has the effect of moving the experience of the poem closer to that of conversation or of ritual. Anglo-Saxon root words, contractions, enjambment, lack of rhyme or slant rhyme or irregular rhyme, all make a poem more conversational; Latin root words, end-stopped lines, regular and true rhyme, all make the experience of a poem closer to that of ritual.

The poet's medium is language as the sculptor's is stone. A poet can't do much to change what words mean, but can do a great deal to change the way they rub up against one another. A part of what we go to poetry for is the soundplay, that is, the rhythms and the way consonants knock together and vowels wrap around them.

And I should also say something about what we mean by a *line* of poetry. A ragged right margin obviously does not turn prose into poetry. The right margin is uneven because a poem is written in lines, and lines are self-defining; we can't decide when we want them to break. A line of poetry is at its best a unit of sense, syntax and rhythm all at the same time. (Note that the unity of sense is violated once in "Adjusting to the Light," in the third line, which breaks after the first word of a sentence to suggest the confusion of the speaker.)

All of the elements I've mentioned can, I hope, be seen at work in both of the accompanying poems.

Let's take a closer look at "Adjusting to the Light."

The alliterative "Lazarus, listen" is intended to focus not only the attention of Lazarus, but of the readers, a way of saying, "Those six lines were the introduction; now that you know where we are, let's get on with the meat of the poem." And then the line announces "things" to follow, raising that expectation and sending the readers forward.

Then we learn that Lazarus, not having lost his life, has lost his sheep, his dog, his sweetheart, his lyre and probably his entire place in the scheme of things. All the while, we move forward from lines like "Rebecca, who cried two days, has given her hand . . ." (to whom?) and discover the answer in a line that then ends with "Please understand . . ." (understand what?), taking us to the next line to find that answer in turn. Sometimes the expectation is subtler, as in "give us time to think" (about what?). And ". . . but you do stink" (what are you going to do about it?). "And one thing more," though, raises very explicitly an expectation of something to follow.

Not every line can raise such questions, of course, and in any case it's not something readers should be conscious of during the reading. But the continual raising and filling of expectations in this way creates the sense of forward motion that readers feel, and creates the energy behind that movement.

Rhyme is absent as the words of Lazarus open the poem. I don't think I could believe his gasping confusion were it expressed in rhyme. The explanation by the sisters becomes increasingly marked by rhyme as they choose their words carefully and look for an order they don't quite find. It slips away from them as the rhyme slips away, never falling into a pattern until the closing strophe, when they apologize and promise to make amends and welcome Lazarus back as best they can; here the terminal rhymes tumble over one another, suggesting, perhaps, that there is still a way to fashion some sort of desperate order here.

Still, Lazarus and the readers both see that he can never truly be at home again. Not as he was. And that every player on the stage has lost something. Time has moved in the wrong direction and will now always be out of joint. Maybe the poem says that miracles are not something to hope for, after all. It is, in any event, a questioning of what we have taken for granted.

"An August Evening Outside of Nashville" seems to be a different poem in almost every element, but it also is a questioning. The lines are still units of sense, syntax and rhythm, and the lines still raise questions that are answered by those that follow. "Seeing a chipmunk in the yard" (doing what?); "hearing the wild bees grow loud" (while what?); "I can almost forget" (forget what?).

But this poem is considerably more formal than the other. This is perhaps because it seems to be in my own voice, and I feel a need for the distance of ritual — in part because I'm a rather private person, but mostly because I want the poem to be *a* love poem, not *my* love poem.

How is the poem a questioning? Well, it's a love poem of 18 lines in which the beloved doesn't show up until line 17, and then with dirty feet. It means to do violence to our stock images of romance and the inward focus of conventional love-talk. Here is a man who, we must assume, has recently been in bed with a woman who is important to him, but his attention is held by beasts and birds and rotting vegetation. Could it be that the love and the act of love have made him somehow more sensitive to the world around him, perhaps larger of mind and spirit?

"I can almost forget. . . ." Does he want to forget? Is the memory a burden to him?

Of course the memory is a burden to him. Every commitment to another human being is a burden. We take up such burdens willingly, but they are burdens nonetheless. Without them we would be freer — freer to charge what we want on the credit card and to have what we want for dinner without wondering whether someone else will like it — but we would be far less human.

It matters in the poem that these people are not married, else he could not be looking for ways to forget her. How do we know they are not married? Because a married man does not speak of "my . . . sheet." But how could this be so if I am the speaker, and I've been married to the same woman for more than a quarter of a century? Well, I lied. An earlier poem of mine about writing poems says, "Invent whatever will support your line. Leave out the rest." Or, as John Ciardi paraphrased Picasso, "Poetry lies its way to the truth." So the poem is not *my* love poem, after all, but *a* love poem. It may even be spoken by a woman to a man.

So what does the poem mean, then? That question, again, should also be, "How does the poem mean?" It means a number of things in a number of ways. A part of what and how it means will depend on who reads it, because a good reader takes part in the completion of a poem; whatever a poem is, finally, belongs in part to each of its readers. The poet James Whitehead and I were invited to Plains, Georgia, in 1981 to help welcome home from Washington Jimmy and Rosalynn Carter, and were asked if we would each write a poem for the occasion. After we read our poems to the Carters in the presence of their assembled family and friends, Mr. Carter accepted presentation copies and spoke briefly. As well as I can recall, he said this to us:

"Rosalynn and I will always keep these poems on our closet wall so that we can read them over and over until we find what is to be found there. Now, what we find may not be only what you put there; it may also be what we took there, because that's what good poetry demands and allows."

I was impressed, first, that we had had a president who was capable of having and framing such thoughts. And then I was impressed by how much of the nature of poetry he had captured.

I have read "The Love Song of J. Alfred Prufrock" many times, but I have never read it twice as the same poem. Because part of what it is I bring to it, and I'm never quite the person who read it before. This is what Mr. Carter understood.

So the meaning of each of these small poems, "Adjusting to the Light" and "An August Evening Outside of Nashville," depends in good part on my co-author—you, the reader—who will bring to them your own memories and associations, attitudes toward myth and religion and nature, your own sense of irony, and the name and ways of your own lover. A poem is not complete until a reader brings these things to it. I will never see these as complete poems; only you can do that. So, in a very real way, it's for *you* to tell *me* what they mean.

SHARON OARD WARNER

THE WAY WE WRITE NOW: THE REALITY OF AIDS IN CONTEMPORARY SHORT FICTION

STUDIES IN SHORT FICTION

She knew as much about this disease as she could know.

The line comes from "Philostorgy, Now Obscure," a short story first published in *The New Yorker*. Its author, Allen Barnett, died of AIDS in 1992. The "disease" the line refers to is, in fact, AIDS, and the "she" is a woman named Roxy, who asks her friend Preston whether he intends to go on DHPG.[1] Roxy knows DHPG is a drug used to treat CMV (cytomegalovirus), and that it requires "a catheter inserted into a vein that fed directly into an atrium of his heart." Roxy has done her homework. In her room, Preston finds "a photocopy of an article from the *New England Journal of Medicine*," as well as "a book on the immune system and one on the crisis published by the National Academy of Sciences, and a list of gay doctors." She has read extensively, and she cares deeply, but there is still much she cannot know. I identify with Roxy: I have read extensively (though not as much as she has), written some, and care deeply, but like her, there is much I cannot know. What I do know, however, I have learned not so much from television documentaries, though I have watched them, and not from articles and reports, though I have read them. What I know about AIDS—about living with it and dying from it—I have learned from literature, from novels and poems and essays, and, most of all, from short stories.

Most of us knew little about AIDS when Susan Sontag's story "The Way We Live Now" was published in 1986 in *The New*

Yorker. "The Way We Live Now" was one of the first stories on AIDS to appear in a mainstream periodical, and it is still—by far—the best known story on the subject. To illustrate, not only was Sontag's story included in *Best American Short Stories 1987*, it was also chosen for the volume *Best American Short Stories of the Eighties*. Last spring, to raise funds for AIDS charities, the story was released once again, this time as a small and expensive volume, complete with illustrations by British artist Howard Hodgkin. In *The New York Times Book Review* (1 March 1992), Gardner McFall proclaimed this newest incarnation of the story "an allegory for our times."

Presumably, the allegorical elements of the story are in what is left out: the name of the main character—the man who is ill—and the name of the disease. These two subjects, person and illness, we learn about through hearsay, second and third hand in a variety of voices:

> I've never spent so many hours at a time on the phone, Stephen said to Kate, and when I'm exhausted after the two or three calls made to me, giving me the latest, instead of switching off the phone to give myself a respite I tap out the number of another friend or acquaintance, to pass on the news.

Surely, one of Ms. Sontag's intentions was "to pass on the news" to the reader. However, the message may not be getting across, at least not to everyone, and perhaps not to those most in need of hearing it. Last fall, I taught "The Way We Live Now" in a fiction writing class at Drake University. Five years had passed since the story's first appearance in *The New Yorker*, a period in which approximately 120,000 Americans died of AIDS. Even so, several students in my class insisted that the disease in question might not be AIDS at all. One young man was adamant; no amount of argument would serve to convince him. Enlightened members of the class pointed to lines such as this one: "Ellen replied, . . . my gynecologist says that everyone is at risk, everyone who has a sexual life, because sexuality is a chain that links each of us to so many others, unknown others, and now the great chain of being has become a chain of death as well." But the student would not be persuaded; he simply preferred to believe that Sontag intended some other disease — any other disease. The meaning of the allegory, if indeed "The Way We Live Now" is an allegory, was certainly lost on this student.

While Sontag's story may well have been the first to avoid the name of the illness, it certainly was not the last. The first volume of stories on AIDS, *A Darker Proof*, by Edmund White and Adam Mars-Jones, mentions the acronym only once in 233 pages. In the foreword to his newest collection of stories, *Monopolies of Loss*, Mars-Jones comments that the "suppression" of the term in the earlier book was intentional.[2] My own experience with writing about AIDS is similar. In writing a story about a foster mother to a baby with AIDS, I deliberately sidestepped the term until page 6, and thereafter used it only twice. My concern was that editors and readers would be turned off by the subject, so I made sure my audience was well into the story before I divulged the truth. Even in fiction, it seems, we are invested in keeping AIDS a secret.

But more problematic than avoiding the name of the illness is the practice of evading the person with AIDS. In Sontag's story, we never learn the man's name — or much else about him, for that matter — except that he has a large number of devoted and talkative friends. In a very real sense, Sontag's story has no main character. What it has, instead, is, at best, a subject of conversation, at worst, grist for the gossip mill. As several of my students pointed out, "The Way We Live Now" is reminiscent of the children's game, "Telephone," in which players sit in a circle and whisper a message in turn:

> At first he was just losing weight, he felt only a little ill, Max said to Ellen, and he didn't call for an appointment with his doctor, according to Greg, because he was managing to keep on working at more or less the same rhythm, but he did stop smoking, Tanya pointed out, which suggests he was frightened, but also that he wanted, even more than he knew, to be healthy, or healthier, or maybe just to gain back a few pounds, said Orson. . . .

This technique is catchy, but it may well cast suspicion on the veracity of what is at hand. After all, the charm of the children's game comes from the inevitable distortion of the message. (If everyone reported correctly, what fun would it be?) Were it only one of many stories on AIDS, the issues of technique and omitted names might be simply matters to be hashed out among literary critics; but, in fact, "The Way We Live Now" continues to be the best-known story on the topic and one of the few to have been published in a commercial periodical.

By and large, the stories about AIDS that have followed Sontag's have also kept their distance from the subject. (Here, I am speaking of stories that have been published in mainstream literary and commercial publications.) As good as these stories are — and some are excellent — most of them are not stories about people with AIDS — instead, they are stories about people who know other people with AIDS. Once again, the disease and those who suffer from it are kept at a distance.

The main characters in these stories tend to be siblings or friends of people living with AIDS. Three good examples are "Close" by Lucia Nevai, which appeared in *The New Yorker* in 1988; "A Sister's Story," by Virginia DeLuca, which appeared in *The Iowa Review* in 1991; and "Nothing to Ask For," by Dennis McFarland, which appeared in *The New Yorker* in 1989 and was later included in *Best American Short Stories 1990*. Guilt plays a major role in all three. While a friend or a sibling struggles with AIDS, the main characters of these stories struggle with feelings.

In Nevai's story, a social worker named Jorie is flying home for the funeral of her brother Jan, "who had contracted AIDS seven months earlier and had not let anyone in the family know." Jan's lover Hank cared for him, "made sure he never lacked for visitors," "made sure he had painkillers," "helped him write a will." The pain of knowing that she was intentionally excluded from the last months of Jan's life is hard for Jorie to bear, but by the end of the story she realizes that "pain was stronger, pain was hungrier. Pain would win this one."

DeLuca's story also concerns a sister whose brother dies. Much of "A Sister's Story" is told through journal entries, and the effect of this technique is the same sort of distance one feels in Sontag's story. As in Nevai's story, the sister is burdened with guilt, partly because her husband is afraid of AIDS, and therefore afraid of her brother, Mike. At one point, the sister confesses her husband's fears to Mike. His response is rage: "Mike turns to me. 'You shouldn't be married to him. Leave him. How can you stay married to him when he does this to me? LEAVE HIM.'" A few days later, the sister writes in her journal that her brother will die faster as a result of the pain she has caused him. Near the end of the story, she writes of her own pain: "So these memories, coming at unexpected times, . . . are like cramps, sudden, fierce, doubling me over—forcing me to clench my jaw."

Of the stories about people who know people with AIDS, "Nothing to Ask For" gets closest to both the illness and those who suffer from it. In the Contributor's Notes of *Best American Short Stories 1990*, Dennis McFarland explains that "Nothing to Ask For" is based on a visit he paid to a close friend just weeks before the friend died of AIDS. He admits that he had trouble with the narrator: "It was hard to let the story be his, while never allowing his concerns to upstage those of the characters who were dying." Perhaps because upstaging was a concern, McFarland's story succeeds in allowing "the horror of the disease to speak for itself." The result is a story full of reverence for life and for those in the midst of leaving it.

The main character of "Nothing to Ask For" is a man named Dan who is spending the day with his friend Mack, who is close to death, and with Mack's lover, Lester, also sick with AIDS. Guilt is an issue in this story as well. At one point, Lester finds Dan in the bathroom sprinkling Ajax around the rim of the toilet bowl:

> "Oh, Dan, really," he [Lester] says. "You go too far. Down on your knees now, scrubbing our toilet."
> "Lester, leave me alone," I say.
> "Well, it's true," he says. "You really do."
> "Maybe I'm working on my survivor's guilt," I say, "if you don't mind."
> "You mean because your best buddy's dying and you're not?"
> "Yes," I say. "It's very common."

He parks one hip on the sink, and after a moment he says this: "Danny boy, if you feel guilty about surviving . . . that's not irreversible, you know. I could fix that."

We are both stunned. He looks at me. In another moment, there are tears in his eyes.

McFarland takes pains to develop both Lester and Mack as characters in their own right. To do so, he pulls us directly into their lives, bypassing gossip, memories, and journal entries.

In order to prepare Dan for the sight of him naked in the bath, Mack calls out, "Are you ready for my Auschwitz look?" As Dan bathes him, Mack muses on his fate: "You know, Dan, it's only logical that they've all given up on me. And I've accepted it mostly. But I still have days when I think I should at least be given a chance." A chance is what McFarland gives this character—the chance to express himself, to enter our psyches, to change us in a way hearsay can never do.

As one might predict, most of the writing about AIDS is being done by gay writers, but readers may not realize that most of this writing is published in collections marketed primarily to gay readers. Not until I began searching out stories dealing with AIDS did I begin to realize just how segregated that market is. A number of the stories I wanted to read were unavailable in local bookstores—even in the bigger and better ones—and the books had to be special-ordered. Others were available in a special section set aside for gay readers. So I was not surprised to find that of the 20 entries under the subject heading "AIDS" in the *Short Story Index* for 1990, eight were published in an anthology called *Men on Men 3*. Four were published in a collection by Allen Barnett called *The Body and Its Dangers*, which I could not locate in libraries or bookstores, despite the fact that the book won a PEN/Hemingway award. The eight remaining were either reprints—McFarland's and Sontag's—or stories appearing in individual collections. Not one of the stories in the 1990 listing appeared in a periodical of any kind. Because few people outside the gay community are exposed to these stories, few are reading them. And we all need to be reading them. These are the stories that go to the heart of the matter, stories by writers who are either HIV-positive themselves or who know enough to risk writing from the point of view of someone with AIDS.

The Darker Proof: Stories From a Crisis was the first collection of fiction dealing with AIDS.[3] It includes four stories by the British writer Adam Mars-Jones and three long stories by American novelist Edmund White. These stories plunge right in, no intermediaries or second-hand information. For instance, Mars-Jones's story, "Slim," begins this way:

> I don't use that word. I've heard it enough. So I've taken it out of circulation, just here, just at home. I say Slim instead, and Buddy understands. I have got Slim. When Buddy pays a visit, I have to remind myself not to offer him a cushion. Most people don't need cushions; they're just naturally covered. So I keep all the cushions to myself, now that I've lost my upholstery.
>
> Slim is what they call it in Uganda, and it's a perfectly sensible name. You lose more weight than you thought was possible. You lose more weight than you could carry. Not that you feel like carrying anything.

Of the 20 stories in *Men on Men 3*, eight are concerned with AIDS. All are well worth reading, but by far the best is Part One of *Halfway Home* by Paul Monette. Though actually an excerpt from a novel, Monette's piece works remarkably well as a piece of short fiction. Monette is a versatile man—a poet, essayist, screenwriter, and novelist—and one of the finest writers I have read in years. His book, *Borrowed Time: An AIDS Memoir*, was nominated for the National Book Critics Circle Award in 1988.[4] It is the intensely moving account of the life and death of Roger Horwitz. In *Borrowed Time*, Monette remarks that "families do not always come together neatly in a tragedy" and Part One of *Halfway Home* is a poignant illustration of this sad truth.

Tom Shaheen is in his early thirties and has not seen his brother Brian in nine years, not since their father's funeral. He fully expects to die without seeing his brother again, and he fully expects to die soon. Until then, he lives in a bungalow by the sea, rent-free courtesy of a gentle and unassuming man named

Gray Baldwin. Every day Tom makes his way slowly down the 80 rickety steps — "my daily encounter with what I've lost in stamina" — to the entrance to a cave by the surf. There, he broods over "missed chances" and "failures of nerve." He does not, however, probe the painful tooth of his childhood — his "scumbag drunk" of a father, his "whimpering" mother. In particular, he avoids thinking about his older brother Brian — beautiful as a Greek god, ruthless as a terrorist. Monette prepares the reader carefully for an unexpected visit, but he is such a skillful writer that Brian's abrupt entrance still takes us by surprise. The encounter is brutal. Monette does not spare Tommy or Brian or the reader. Guilt is an issue here, too, but now we see it from the other side of the gun. When Brian tries to say he is sorry, Tommy feels not forgiveness but the added burden of his brother's regret:

> Suddenly I feel drained, almost weepy, but not for Brian's sake. . . . The whole drama of coming out — the wrong-headed yammer, the hard acceptance — seems quaint and irrelevant now. Perhaps I'd prefer my brother to stay a pig, because it's simpler. And even though he's not the Greek god he used to be, fleshier now and slightly ruined, I feel *more* sick and frail in his presence. Not just because of AIDS, but like I'm the nerd from before too. "You can't understand," I say, almost a whisper. "All my friends have died."

Part One of *Halfway Home* cannot be neatly summed up. It is not simply a story about a confrontation between two brothers, a story about AIDS, or self-pity, or a growing acceptance of death. It is about all these things plus so many others. As George Stambolian explains in the Introduction to *Men on Men 3*, "The epidemic . . . challenges and tests our beliefs, makes time directly perceptible to our hearts and minds." He goes on to quote Robert Gluck: "Now death is where gay men . . . learn about love. . . ." And love is a subject Monette knows more about than any other contemporary writer I can think of. Near the end of the story, Tommy steals into the bedroom where his brother is sleeping. Looking down at Brian, Tommy feels intense hate —

"I'm like a bad witch, rotten with curses, casting a spell even I can't see the end of" — and bitter love:

> I take a last long look at Brian, and on impulse I lean above him, hover over his face and brush my lips against his cheek. . . . I've never kissed my brother before. He doesn't flinch, he doesn't notice. Then I turn and stumble back to my room, pleading the gods to be rid of him.

While I was working on my own story about AIDS, a writer friend advised me to change the disease. "I really like this story," she told me, "but why does the baby have to have AIDS?" I had no answer for that question, really. Why does anyone have to have AIDS? The impetus for my story was something I overheard about a single woman in Chicago who nurses babies with AIDS. When one child dies, she simply turns to caring for another. After hearing about that brave woman, I wanted to get to know her, and because I am a fiction writer, that meant writing a story. While I could change many things about "A Simple Matter of Hunger," I could not change the disease. That much, at least, I am sure of.

The tragedy is that babies do have AIDS, that an estimated one million people in the US are infected with the HIV virus. According to the Centers for Disease Control, by the end of 1995, the USA will have at least 415,000 AIDS cases and at least 330,000 AIDS deaths. It is not something we can avoid as writers, as readers, or as human beings. "But I was taught not to write about social issues," my friend explained to me. "They just don't last. In a hundred years, it's possible that AIDS may be completely forgotten." We can hope for that, I suppose, but it does not change the present. Right now, we all need to know as much about this disease as we can know.

Ms. Sontag ends "The Way We Live Now" this way: "I was thinking, Ursala said to Quentin, that the difference between a story and a painting or a photograph is that in a story you can write, He's still alive. But in a painting or a photo you can't show 'still.' You can just show him being alive. He's still alive, Stephen said." Ironically, in this most famous story about AIDS, "he" whoever he might be, isn't *shown* still alive. For that, we have to take Stephen's word. And while his word might have been enough to begin with, now and in the future we will need something more. We will need stories like Monette's, stories whose main characters speak to us directly: "I've been at this thing for a year and a half, three if you count all the fevers and rashes. I operate on the casual assumption that I've still got a couple of years, give or take a galloping lymphoma. Day to day, I'm not a dying man, honestly." See there, Tom Shaheen is still alive. Take it from Monette, someone who knows.

[1] To invoke the acronym AIDS is to call forth a whole legion of acronyms: HIV, ARC, PCP, AZT, KS, FDA, CDC — but you get the idea.

[2] Adam Mars-Jones's collection, *Monopolies of Loss*, includes all four stories from *The Darker Proof* plus four new stories dealing with AIDS.

[3] Allen Barnett's collection, *The Body and Its Dangers* (1990), also deals extensively with AIDS. And in 1993, two new collections on the subject have appeared — Adam Mars-Jones's *Monopolies of Loss* and Jameson Currier's *Dancing on the Moon: Short Stories About AIDS* (Viking). The first story in Currier's collection, "What They Carried," borrows much in terms of structure and technique from Tim O'Brien's "The Things They Carried," and from Susan Sontag's "The Way We Live Now." It is also worth noting that only one story in *Dancing on the Moon* is written from the viewpoint of a character with AIDS. The main characters in the other stories are lovers, relatives, and friends, some of whom may be HIV-positive.

[4] Paul Monette received the 1992 National Book Award in non-fiction for *Becoming a Man: Half a Life Story*.

LORRIE MOORE

BETTER AND SICKER

THE AGONY AND THE EGO: THE ART AND STRATEGY OF FICTION
WRITING EXPLORED, EDITED BY CLARE BOYLAN

Recently I received a letter from an acquaintance in which he said, "By the way, I've been following and enjoying your work. It's getting better: deeper and sicker."

Because the letter was handwritten, I convinced myself, for a portion of the day, that perhaps the last word was *richer*. But then I picked up the letter and looked at the word again: there was the *s*, there was the *k*. There was no denying it. Even though denial had been my tendency of late. I had recently convinced myself that a note I'd received from an ex-beau (in what was a response to my announcement that I'd gotten married) had read "Best Wishes for Oz." I considered this an expression of bitterness on my ex-beau's part, a snide lapse, a doomed man's view of marriage, and it gave me great satisfaction. *Best Wishes for Oz.* Eat your heart out, I thought. You had your chance. Cry me a river. Later a friend, looking at the note, pointed out that, "Look: This isn't an O. This is a nine — see the tail? And this isn't a Z. This is a 2. This says 92. 'Best Wishes for 92.'" It hadn't been cryptic bitterness at all — only an indifferent little New Year's greeting. How unsatisfying!

So now when I looked at *deeper and richer*, I knew I had to be careful not to misread wishfully. The phrase wasn't, finally, *deeper and richer*; it was deeper and *sicker*. My work was deeper and sicker.

But what did that mean, *sicker*, and why or how might this adjective be applied in a friendly manner? I wasn't sure. But it brought me to thinking of the things that I had supposed fiction was supposed to be, what art was supposed to be, what writers and artists were supposed to do, and whether it could possibly include some aesthetics of sickness.

I think it's a common thing for working writers to go a little blank when asking themselves too many fundamental questions about what it is they're doing. Some of this has to do with the lost perspective that goes with being so immersed. And some of it has to do with just plain not having a clue. Of course, this is the curse of the grant application, for instance, which includes that hilarious part called the project description (describe in detail the book you are going to write) wherein you are asked to know the unknowable, and if not to know it then just to say it anyway for cash. That a grant-giving agency would trust a specific and detailed description from a fiction writer seems sweetly naive—though fiction writers are also allowed to file their own taxes, write their own parents, sign their own checks, raise their own children—so it is a tolerant and generous or at least innocent world here and there.

What writers do is workmanlike: tenacious, skilled labour. That we know. But it is also mysterious. And the mystery involved in the act of creating a narrative is attached to the mysteries of life itself, and the creation of life itself: that we are; that there is *something* rather than *nothing*. Though I wonder whether it sounds preposterous in this day and age to say such a thing. No one who has ever looked back upon a book she or he has written, only to find the thing foreign and alienating, unrecallable, would ever deny this mysteriousness. One can't help but think that in some way this surprise reflects the appalled senility of God herself, or himself, though maybe it's the weirdly paired egotism and humility of artists that leads them over and over again to this creational cliché: that we are God's dream, God's characters; that literary fiction is God's compulsion handed down to us, an echo, a diminishment, but something we are made to do in imitation, perhaps even in honour, of that original creation, and made to do in understanding of what flimsy vapours we all are—though also how heartbreaking and amusing. In more scientific terms, the compulsion to read and write—and it seems to me it should be, even must be, a compulsion—is a bit of mental wiring the species has selected, over time, in order, as the life span increases, to keep us interested in ourselves.

For it's crucial to keep ourselves, as a species, interested in ourselves. When that goes, we tip into the void, we harden to rock, we blow away and disappear. Art has been given to us to keep us interested and engaged—rather than distracted by materialism or sated with boredom—so that we can attach to this life, a life that might, otherwise, be an unbearable one.

And so, perhaps, it is this compulsion to keep ourselves interested that can make the work seem, well, a little sick. (I'm determined, you see, if not to read *sicker* as *richer* then at least to read *sicker* as OK.) Certainly so much of art originates and locates itself within the margins, that is, the contours, of the human self, as a form of locating and defining that self. And certainly art, and the life of the artist, requires a goodly amount of shamelessness. The route to truth and beauty is a toll road—tricky and unpretty in and of itself.

But are the impulses toward that journey pathological ones?

I took inventory of my own life.

Certainly as a child, I had done things that now seem like clues indicating I was headed for a life that was not quite normal—one that was perhaps "artistic." I detached things: the charms from bracelets, the bows from dresses. This was a time—the early sixties, an outpost, really, of the fifties—when little girls' dresses had lots of decorations: badly stitched appliqué, or little plastic berries, lace flowers, satin bows. I liked to remove them and would often then re-attach them—on a sleeve or a mitten. I liked to re-contextualize even then—one of the symptoms. Other times, I would just collect these little detached things and play with them, keeping them in a little bowl in a dresser drawer in my room. If my dresses had been denuded, made homely, it didn't matter to me: I had a supply of lovely little gew-gaws in a bowl. I had begun a secret life. A secret harvest. I had begun perhaps a kind of literary life—one that would continue to wreak havoc on my wardrobe, but, alas, those are the dues. I had become a magpie, collecting shiny objects. I was a starling in reverse: building a nest under eggs gathered from here and there.

When I was a little older, say eleven or twelve, I used to sit on my bed with a sketch pad, listening to songs on the radio. Each song would last three to four minutes, and during that time, I would draw the song: I would draw the character I imagined was singing the song, and the setting that character was in — usually there were a lot of waves and seagulls, docks and coastlines. I lived in the mountains, away from the oceans, but a babysitter I'd had when I was nine had taught me how to draw lighthouses, so I liked to stick in a lighthouse whenever possible. After one song was over, I'd turn the page and draw the next one, filling notebooks this way. I was obsessed with songs — songs and letters (I had a pen-pal in Canada) — and I often think that that is what I tried to find later in literature: the feeling of a song; the friendly, confiding voice of a letter but the cadence and feeling of a song. When a piece of prose hit rhythms older, more familiar and enduring than itself, it seemed then briefly to belong to nature, or at least to the world of music, and that's when it seemed to me "artistic" and good.

I exhibited other signs of a sick life — a strange, elaborate crush on Bill Bixby, a belief in a fairy godmother, also a bit of journalism my brother and I embarked on called Mad Man Magazine, which consisted of our writing on notebook paper a lot of articles we'd make up about crazy people, especially crazy people in haunted houses, then tying the pages together with ribbon and selling them to family members for a nickel. But it was a life of the imagination.

When I was older, I suppose there were other signs of sickness. I preferred hearing about parties to actually going to them. I liked to phone the next day and get the news from a friend. I wanted gossip, third-handedness; narrative. My reading was scattered, random, unsystematic. I wasn't one of these nice teenaged girls who spent their summers reading all of Jane Austen. My favourite books were *The Great Gatsby* by F. Scott Fitzgerald and *Such Good Friends* by Lois Gould. Later, like so many (of the "afflicted"), I discovered the Brontës. One enters these truly great, truly embarrassing books like a fever dream — in fact, fever dreams figure prominently in them. They are situated in sickness, and unafraid of that. And that's what made them wonderful to me. They were at the centre of something messy. But they didn't seem foreign in the least. In fact, very little written by a woman seemed foreign to me. Books by women came as great friends, a relief. They showed up on the front lawn and waved. Books by men one had to walk a distance to get to, take a hike to arrive at, though as readers we girls were all well-trained for the hike and we didn't learn to begrudge and resent it until later. A book by a woman, a book that began up close, on the heart's porch, was a treat, an exhilaration, and finally, I think, that is why women who became writers did so: to create more books in the world by women; to give themselves something more to read.

When I first started writing, I often felt sorry for men, especially white men, for it seemed the reasons for their becoming writers was not so readily apparent, or compelling, but had to be searched for, even made excuses for. Though their quote-unquote tradition was so much more celebrated and available, it was also more filled up. It was ablaze. What did a young male writer feel he was adding? As a woman, I never felt that. There seemed to be a few guiding lights (I, of course, liked the more demented ones — Sexton, Plath, McCullers), but that was enough. Admiration and enthusiasm and a sense of scarcity: inspiration without the anxiety of influence.

I feel a little less like that now, in part because I know the main struggle for every writer is with the dance and limitations of language — to honour the texture of it but also to make it unafraid. One must throw all that one is into language, like a Christmas tree hurled into a pool. One must listen and proceed, sentence to sentence, hearing what comes next in one's story — which can be a little maddening. It can be like trying to understand a whisper in a foreign accent: did she say *Je t'adore* or *Shut the door?*

To make the language sing while it works is a task to one side of gender. How often I've tried to shake from my own storytelling the phrase *And then suddenly*, as if I could wake up a story with the false drama of those three words. It's usually how I know my writing's going badly; I begin every sentence that way:

And then suddenly he went to the store. And then suddenly the store was brick. And then suddenly he had been asleep for eight hours. The writer marries the language, said Auden, and out of this marriage writing is born. But what if the language feels inadequate, timid, recalcitrant, afraid? I often think of the Albert Goldbarth poem "Alien Tongue" wherein the poet thinks wistfully, adulterously of an imagined language parsed to such a thinness that there is a tense that means "I would have if I'd been my twin." What an exquisite, precision tool such a tense would be for a writer! Whole rooms could be added to scenes; whole paragraphs to pages; books to books; sequels where at first there were no sequels. . . . But then excessive literary production, George Eliot reminds us, is a social offence. As far as language goes we have to live contentedly, and discontentedly, with our own, making it do what it can, and also, a little of what it can't. And this contradiction brings one back, I suppose, to a makeshift aesthetics of sickness.

Writing is both the excursion into and the excursion out of one's life. That is the queasy paradox of the artistic life. It is the thing that, like love, removes one both painfully and deliciously from the ordinary shape of existence. It joins another queasy paradox: that life is both an amazing, hilarious, blessed gift and that it is also intolerable. Even in the luckiest life, for example, one loves someone and then that someone dies. This is not *acceptable*. This is a major design flaw! To say nothing of the world's truly calamitous lives. The imagination is meant outwardly to console us with all that is interesting, not so much to subtract but to add to our lives. It reminds me of a progressive Italian elementary school I read of once in which the classrooms had two dress-up areas with trunks of costumes—just in case, while studying math or plants, a child wanted to be in disguise that day.

But the imagination also forces us inward. It constructs inwardly from what has entered our inwardness. The best art, especially literary art, embraces the very idea of paradox: it sees opposites, antitheses co-existing. It sees the blues and violets, in a painting of an orange; it sees the scarlets and the yellows in a bunch of Concord grapes. In narrative, tones share space — often queasily, the ironies quivering. Consider these lines from the Alice Munro story, "A Real Life": "Albert's heart had given out — he had only had time to pull to the side of the road and stop the truck. He died in a lovely spot, where black oaks grew in a bottomland, and a sweet, clear creek ran beside the road." Or these lines from a Garrison Keillor monologue: "And so he tasted it, and a look of pleasure came over him, and then he died. Ah, life is good. Life is good." What constitutes tragedy and what constitutes comedy may be a fuzzy matter. The comedienne Joan Rivers has said that there isn't any suffering that's one's own that isn't also potentially very funny. Delmore Schwartz claimed that the only way anyone could understand *Hamlet* was to assume right from the start that all the characters were roaring drunk. I often think of an acquaintance of mine who is also a writer and whom I ran into once in a bookstore. We exchanged hellos, and when I asked her what she was working on these days, she said, "Well, I *was* working on a long comic novel, but then in the middle of the summer my husband had a terrible accident with an electric saw and lost three of his fingers. It left us so sad and shaken that when I returned to writing, my comic novel kept getting droopier, darker and sadder and depressing. So I scrapped it, and started writing a novel about a man who loses three fingers in an accident with a saw, and *that*," she said, "*that's* turning out to be really funny."

A lesson in comedy.

Which leads one also to that paradox, or at least that paradoxical term "autobiographical fiction." Fiction writers are constantly asked, is this autobiographical? Book reviewers aren't asked this; and neither are concert violinists, though, in my opinion, there is nothing more autobiographical than a book review or a violin solo. But because literature has always functioned as a means by which to figure out what is happening to us, as well as what we think about it, fiction writers do get asked: "What is the relationship of this story/novel/play to the events of your own life (whatever they may be)?"

I *do* think that the proper relationship of a writer to his or her own life is similar to a cook with a cupboard. What that cook makes from what's in the cupboard is not the same thing as what's in the cupboard — and of course, everyone understands that. Even in the most autobiographical fiction there is a kind of *paraphrase* going on, which is Katherine Ann Porter's word, and which is a good one for use in connection with her, but also for general use. I personally have never written autobiographically in the sense of using and transcribing events from my life. None — or at least very few — of the things that have happened to my characters have ever happened to me. But one's life is there constantly collecting and providing and it will creep into one's work regardless — in emotional ways. I often think of a writing student I had once who was blind. He never once wrote about a blind person — never wrote about blindness at all. But he wrote about characters who constantly bumped into things, who tripped, who got bruised; and that seemed to me a very true and very characteristic transformation of life into art. He wanted to imagine a person other than himself; but his journey toward that person was *paradoxically* and necessarily through his own life. Like a parent with children, he gave his characters a little of what he knew — but not everything. He nurtured rather than replicated or transcribed.

Autobiography can be a useful tool: it coaxes out the invention — actually invention and autobiography coax out each other; the pen takes refuge from one in the other, looking for moral dignity and purpose in each, and then flying to the arms of the other. All the energy that goes into the work, the force of imagination and concentration, *is* a kind of autobiographical energy, no matter what one is actually writing about. One has to give to one's work like a lover. One must give of oneself, and try not to pick fights. Perhaps it *is* something of a sickness — halfway between "quarantine and operetta" (to steal a phrase from Celine) — to write intensely, closely — not with one's pen at arm's length, but perhaps with one's arm out of the way entirely, one's hand up under one's arm, near the heart, thrashing out like a flipper, one's face hovering close above the page, listening with ear and cheek, lips forming the words. Martha Graham speaks of the Icelandic term "doom eager" to denote that ordeal of isolation, restlessness, caughtness and artistic experiences when he or she is sick with an idea.

When a writer is doom eager, the writing won't be sludge on the page; it will give readers—and the writer, of course, is the very first reader—an experience they've never had before, or perhaps a little and at last the words for an experience they have. The writing will disclose a world; it will be that Heideggerean "setting-itself-into-work of the truth of what it is." But it will not have lost the detail; detail, on its own, contains the universe. As Flannery O'Conner said, "It's always necessary to remember that the fiction writer is much less immediately concerned with grand ideas . . . than he is with putting list slippers on clerks." One must think of the craft—that impulse to make an object from the materials lying about, as much as the spiritual longing, the philosophical sweep. "It is impossible to experience one's own death objectively," Woody Allen once said, "and still carry a tune."

Obviously one must keep a certain amount of literary faith, and not be afraid to travel with one's work into margins and jungles and danger zones, and one should also live with someone who can cook and who will both be with one and leave one alone. But there is no formula, to the life or to the work, and all any writer finally knows are the little decisions he or she has been forced to make, given the particular choices. There's no golden recipe. Most things literary are stubborn as colds; they resist all formulas—a chemist's, a wet nurse's, a magician's. Finally, there is no formula outside the sick devotion to the work. Perhaps one would be wise when young even to avoid thinking of oneself as a writer—for there's something a little stopped and satisfied, too healthy, in that. Better to think of *writing*, of what one does as an activity, rather than an identity—to write, I write; we write; to keep the calling a verb rather than a noun; to keep working at the thing, at all hours, in all places, so that your life does not become a pose, a pornography of wishing. William Carlos Williams said, "Catch an eyeful, catch an earful, and don't drop what you've caught." He was a doctor. So presumably he knew about *sicker* and *better* and how they are often quite close.

IMAGINING WHAT YOU DON'T KNOW

THE WRITER

I have been unable to put out of my mind, though I have tried, a sentence I glimpsed in the last paragraph of an interview with a novelist that appeared in a national magazine a few years ago. The novelist, when asked about her plans, replied, "Now that I have succeeded as a writer, I'm looking for new forms of stimulation."

Such fatuousness is not exceptional, perhaps not even surprising during these days when one of the more intrusive catchwords has become *lifestyle*, with its implication that how one lives is entirely by choice, by will, and when the director of a national self-help organization announces from his platform that "We must applaud everything equally and give up the useless habit of evaluation."

Life is not a style, any more than death is a style, although if we give up the "useless habit of evaluation," we may not be able to tell the difference. And as for succeeding as a writer, a claim that in the days of my own youth no writer would have been caught dead making, and wouldn't, I venture to say, have secretly thought, here is what Cesare Pavese says about such self-congratulation in his diary, *This Business of Living*:

Complacency is a deficiency whose penalty is a special perennial adolescence of the spirit. It is doubt which alone can make us probe and glimpse the depth of consciousness.

I have written and published six adult novels and twenty books for young people. Save for an occasional sentence, a paragraph here and there, I haven't been content with my work. "Eased" is closer to describing the sense of deliverance I feel when the last galley is corrected, when I am, for a time, free of the enveloping tension of work.

During those quiet days, a kind of truce prevails in me. I am relatively untroubled, either by doubt or certainty, volatile states in any case. In fact, for a little while, I rest almost in a torpor, its surface only faintly ruffled by mild, vague thoughts. I can hardly recall, in this state, the days of the years when work was like digging a trench in hard ground. I forget the times of confusion, of tedium, of a failure of nerve, of pulling myself together once more to go to my workroom, wishing the telephone would ring, resenting it when it does, wishing for any distraction, yet dreading all distraction. I forget, too, the moments when writing seems nearly effortless (there are few of those!), and a voice seems to speak through me. And I forget the deep pleasure of an absorption so complete that time itself weighs nothing.

Before the book is actually published, any judgment of mine on the possible failure or success of the book I have written bears on how effectively reviewers will encourage or discourage readers from buying it and reading it; the significance of that kind of success or failure is that it will—or will not—result in buying me time so I can begin once again.

The calm is soon over. A few reviews trickle in. A painful prospect opens up. My book will not be understood by anyone. It will not be read by anyone. Or if it is read and written about somewhere, it will be by that same happy and successful novelist whose words I quoted at the start of this article. And she will say about my book: It has not succeeded! Let the writer seek a new form of stimulation!

Hard and unremitting labor is what writing is. It is in that labor that I feel the weight and force of my own life. That is its great and nettlesome reward.

It is not easy to convince people who take writing courses just how much labor is required of a writer.

After all, their mouths are full of words. They need only transfer those words to paper. Writing can't be really difficult, like learning to play the oboe, for example, or studying astrophysics.

Pavese, in his diary, also writes:

> They say that to create while actually writing is to reach out beyond whatever plan we have made, searching, listening to the deep truth within. But often the profoundest truth we have is the plan we have created by slow, ruthless, weary effort and surrender.

Most students of writing need little convincing about the deep truth they have within them, but they are not always partial to "slow, ruthless, weary effort." Few of us are. Yet there comes a time when you know that ruthless effort is what you must exert. There is no other way. And on that way you will discover such limitations in yourself as to make you gasp. But you work on. If you have done that for a long time, something will happen. You will succeed in becoming dogged. You will become resolute about one thing: to go to your desk day after day and try. You will give up the hope that you can come to a conclusion about yourself as a writer. You will give up conclusions.

The English critic, John Middleton Murry, wrote:

> A writer does not really come to conclusions about life, he discovers a quality in it. His emotions, reinforcing one another, gradually form in him a habit of emotion; certain kinds of objects and incidents impress him with a peculiar weight and significance. This emotional bias or predilection is what I have ventured to call the writer's mode of experience; it is by virtue of this mysterious accumulation of past emotions that the writer, in his maturity, is able to accomplish the miracle of giving to the particular the weight and force of the universal.

People who see themselves as having succeeded so thoroughly at writing that there is nothing left for them except to search out fresh fields of endeavor are not, in my view, in the right profession. Conclusions about life are just what such authors like best. They wish to believe there are answers to everything, and everything is defined by them as that for which they have answers.

I think that the character, the temperament, of their products, exhibit a kind of perverted social-workerism. And their fiction trivializes even as it sentimentalizes our lives no less than did the older, didactic literature of the past, toward which these new didactic writers often express such lofty contempt.

These are not tellers of tales, imaginers. They are answers, like those voices on the telephone, which, for a fee, can provide a caller with a prayer, a joke, sexual stimulation, weather reports, or a list of antidotes in case one has swallowed poison.

In *The Tragic Sense of Life*, Miguel de Unamuno tells of Solon weeping over the death of his son. When asked why he is weeping, since it will avail him nothing, "That," replied Solon, "is why I was weeping."

Complacency is a deadweight on the spirit. It smothers imagination. But one rarely hears talk about imagination, especially in the classroom. This is partly due, I think, to an insidious kind of censorship. Censors have always been around, wanting to ban books because they contain some sexual or social or political content that frightens or repels them.

But the new censors tell us that, as writers, our only valid subject is ourselves, or those identical to ourselves, as though we were clumps of clones distributed about the earth. Men are to write only about men, women about women, black people about black people, and so on.

What a foretaste of the intolerable boredom that lies ahead! What is to be done with Tolstoy's reflective hunting dog, with Gogol's Nose, with Turgenev's singers of the Brezhin meadow, with Sancho Panza's imaginary kingdom, with all the men and women and children and ghosts and gods and animals that have been imagined and made living for us in all the stories that witness and record our pleasures and our sufferings, the mystery of our lives?

Narrowing, ever narrowing, the new censors, their tiny banners inscribed with ominous declarations: *I can't identify with that!*

I can't relate to this! seem to want to ban humanity itself, in all its disarray and difference!

"Maybe we're here," the poet, Rainer Maria Rilke, said, "only to say: house, bridge, well, gate, jug, olive-tree, window — at most, pillar, tower — but to say them, remember, oh! to say them in a way that the things themselves never dreamed of so intensely."

As I write Rilke's words, I think of the great silence into which we hold up our small bundle of words; it is like the blue light of our small planet glimmering in the darkness that is all around.

MY FATHER'S PLACE

HUNGRY MIND REVIEW

A few days after my father, poet William Stafford, died, I was sleeping alone at the house of my parents, when something woke me at around 4 A.M. My mother, who was away, had told me of this effect, for she, too, had been wakened since his death at my father's customary writing time. As I opened my eyes, the moon was shining through the bedroom window. But that wasn't it. The house was still, the neighborhood quiet. The house wanted me to rise. It was the hour, a beckoning. There was a soft tug. Nothing mystical, just a habit to the place. The air was sweet, life was good, it was time.

I dressed, and shuffled down the hall. In the kitchen, I remembered how he would make himself a cup of instant coffee, and some toast. I followed the custom, putting the kettle on, slicing some bread my mother had made, letting the plink of the spoon stirring the coffee be the only sound, then the scrape of the butter knife. And then I was to go to the couch, and lie down with paper. I pulled the green mohair blanket from the closet, turned on a lamp, and settled in the horizontal place where my father had greeted maybe ten thousand mornings with his pen and paper. I put my head on the pillow just where his head had worn through the silk lining.

What should I write? There was no sign, only a feeling of generosity in the room. A streetlight brightened the curtain beside me, but the rest of the room was dark. I let my gaze rove the walls—the fireplace, the dim rectangle of a painting, the hooded box of the television cabinet, a table with magazines. It was all ordinary, suburban. But there was this beckoning. In the dark of the house it felt as if my father's death had become an empty bowl that was filled from below, like the stone cavern of a spring that brimmed cold with water from a deep place. There was grief, and also this abundance. So many people had written to us saying, "Words cannot begin to express how we feel . . ." They can't? I honored the feeling, for I, too, am sometimes mute with grief. But words *can* begin to express how it is, especially if they can be relaxed, brimming in their own plain way.

I looked for a long time at the bouquet of sunflowers on the coffee table beside the couch. I remembered sunflowers are the state flower of Kansas. I remembered my father's poem about yellow cars. I remembered how, the night before, we had eaten the last of his third summer planting of green beans.

For a time, I thought back to the last writing my father had done at this place, the morning of August 28. As often, he had begun with a line from an ordinary experience, a stray call from an insurance agent trying to track down what turned out to be a different William Stafford. The call had amused him, the words had stayed with him. And that morning, he had begun to write:

> "Are you Mr. William Stafford?"
> "Yes, but. . . ."

As often, he started with the recent daily news from his own life, and came to deeper things:

> Well, it was yesterday.
> Sunlight used to follow my hand.
> And that's when the strange
>   siren-like sound flooded
> over the horizon and rushed
>   through the streets of our
>   town. . . .

But I wasn't delving into his writing now, only his writing life. I was inhabiting the cell of his habit: earlier than anyone, more ordinary in this welcome, simply listening.

The house was so quiet, I was aware distinctly of my breathing, my heart, how sweet each breath came into me, and the total release of each exhalation. I felt as if my eyes, too, had been "tapered for braille." The edge of the coffee table held a soft gleam from the streetlight. The jostled stack of magazines had a kind of sacred logic, where he had touched them. Then I saw how each sunflower had dropped a little constellation of pollen on the table. The pollen seemed to burn, so intense in color and purpose. But the house — the house didn't want me to write anything profound. The soft tug that had wakened me, the tug I still felt, wanted me to be there with myself, awake, awake to everything ordinary, to sip my bitter instant coffee, and to gaze about and to remember. I remembered how my father had said once that such a time alone would allow anyone to go inward, in order to go outward. Paradoxically, he said, you had to go into yourself in order to find the patterns that were bigger than your own life.

I started to write ordinary things. And then I came to the sunflowers, and the spirit of the house warned me this could be told wrong if I tried to make something of it. It's not about trying. It's not about writing poems. It's not about achievement, certainly not fame, importance. It's about being there exactly with the plain life of a time before first light, with breath, the streetlight on one side of the house and the moon on the other, about the worn silk, the blanket, and that little dusting of pollen from the sunflowers.

My head fit the dent in the pillow, the blanket warmed my body, my hand moved easily, carelessly with the pen. I heard the scratch on paper. If this was grieving, it was active in plain things. I found myself relishing the simplest words, mistrusting metaphor, amused by my own habits of verve with words, forgiving myself an occasional big thought:

> . . . to pause at the gate to take
> off the one big shoe
> of his body and step forward light
> as wind . . .

I could forgive myself because there was this abundance in time and place and habit. And then I had a page, I closed my notebook, and I rose for the day. There was much to do, but I had done the big thing already.

Who will take my father's place in the world of poetry? No one. Who will take his place in this daily practice of the language of the tribe? Anyone who wishes. He said once the field of writing will never be crowded—not because people can't do important work, but because they don't think they can. This way of writing beckons to anyone who wishes to rise and listen, to write without fear of either achievement or failure. There is no burden, only a beckoning. For when the house beckons, you will wake easily. There is a stove where you make something warm. There is a light that leaves much of the room dark. There is a place to be comfortable, a place you have worn with the friendly shape of your body. There is your own breath, the treasuries of your recollection, the blessings of your casual gaze. What is this way of writing, of listening easily and telling simply? There is the wall, the table, and whatever stands this day for Kansas pollen in your own precious life.

ABOUT THE AUTHORS

EDWARD ALBEE has published twenty-six plays. Two of his plays—*A Delicate Balance* and *Seascape*—have been awarded the Pulitzer Prize, while his play *Who's Afraid of Virginia Woolf* won a Tony Award. The Off Broadway Signature Theater devoted its 1993-94 season to Albee, performing seven of his plays.

CANDYCE BARNES has published stories in *Story*, *High Plains Literary Review*, *Georgia Review* and *Southern Review*. She recently completed a novel. "Passing the Torch" is taken from a memoir in progress titled *Two Writing Lives*, which she is writing with her husband, Robert Canzoneri.

ANN BEATTIE's most recent novel is *Picturing Will*, published by Random House and reprinted by the Vintage Contemporary Series. Her most recent short story collection, *What Was Mine and Other Stories*, was also published by Random House.

AYANNA BLACK is the editor of *Fiery Spirits* and *Voices*, anthologies of poetry and fiction by Canadian writers of African descent, both published by HarperCollins Canada. She lives in Toronto, Canada, and is working on a new poetry collection titled *Invoking the Spirits*. "Inglish: Writing With an Accent" is based on a lecture she gave at the Visible Minority Conference in Vancouver, British Columbia, Canada.

JAMES FENTON's most recent book is *All the Wrong Places: Adrift in the Politics of the Pacific Rim*, a collection of essays published by Atlantic Monthly Press. He is a columnist for the daily *London Independent*. "Some Mistakes People Make About Poetry" is based on the 1992 Ronald Duncan lecture, delivered in London in association with the Poetry Book Society.

PAULA FOX is the author of numerous novels for adults and for young adults. Her most recent adult novel is *The God of Nightmares*, published by North Point Press, and her most recent young adult novel is *Western Wind*, published by Orchard Books.

DAVID FREEMAN is the author of four books, including *A Hollywood Education: Tales of Movie Dreams and Easy Money*, published by Dell, and *The Last Days of Alfred Hitchcock*, published by Overlook Press. "A Screenwriter's Lexicon" is part of an occasional series titled "A Hollywood Lexicon" that he writes for *The New Yorker*.

BONNIE FRIEDMAN's work has appeared in *The New York Times Book Review*, *River Styx*, *USA Today* and other publications. She received her M.F.A. from the University of Iowa and has taught at Dartmouth College, Northeastern University and the University of Iowa.

ALLAN GURGANUS is the author of *Oldest Living Confederate Widow Tells All*, a novel, and *White People: Stories and Novellas*, both published by Alfred A. Knopf. He has won numerous awards, including the Sue Kaufman Prize, the *Los Angeles Times* Book Prize and the Southern Book Award.

DONALD HALL has published numerous collections of poetry, and his poems have been widely anthologized. His most recent collection is titled *The Museum of Clear Ideas*, published by Ticknor & Fields.

CAROLYN G. HEILBRUN is the author of *Writing a Woman's Life*, published by W.W. Norton, and *Hamlet's Mother and Other Women*, published by Colorado University Press. She is currently writing a biography of Gloria Steinem.

WILLIAM KITTREDGE, who grew up on a large cattle ranch in southeastern Oregon, teaches creative writing at the University of Montana. His most recent book, *Hole in the Sky: A Memoir*, was published by Alfred A. Knopf.

TONY KUSHNER's epic *Angels in America* won the Pulitzer Prize for drama and the Tony Award for best play in 1992. His essay titled "With a Little Help From My Friends" is included with his play *Perestroika* in a volume published by Theater Communications Group.

DIANE LEFER is the author of *The Circles I Move In*, a short story collection published by Zoland Books. She has published several dozen short stories in literary journals and magazines including *The Kenyon Review*, *Redbook*, *The Virginia Quarterly Review* and *Vogue*. A five-time winner of PEN Syndicated Fiction prizes, she has also received grants from the National Endowment for the Arts. She teaches in the M.F.A. program at Vermont College.

MARGOT LIVESEY grew up in Scotland. Her novel, *Homework*, was published by Viking Press. She has taught recently at the Iowa Writers' Workshop, Boston University and Warren Wilson College.

NANCY MAIRS is the author of a number of books, including *Ordinary Time*, published by Beacon Press, *Remembering the Bone House: An Erotics of Place and Space* and *Carnal Acts*, published by HarperCollins. The excerpt titled "The Literature of Personal Disaster" from *Voice Lessons: On Becoming a (Woman) Writer*, published by Beacon Press, appeared originally in *The New York Times Book Review* under the title "When Bad Things Happen to Good Writers."

JAMES MICHENER is the author of numerous bestselling novels. His first novel, *Tales of the South Pacific*, published by Random House, won a Pulitzer Prize. His most recent book is *Literary Reflections*, published by State House Press.

LORRIE MOORE is the author of two collections of stories, *Self-Help* and *Like Life*, both published by NAL-Dutton, and a novel, *Anagrams*, published by Viking Penguin. She teaches creative writing at the University of Wisconsin.

DONALD M. MURRAY writes a weekly column, "Over Sixty," for *The Boston Globe*. He has written several books on the craft of writing, published two novels, and his poetry has appeared in a number of literary journals. He is Professor Emeritus of English at the University of New Hampshire.

JOSIP NOVAKOVICH's short stories and essays have appeared in numerous literary magazines. *Salvation and Other Disasters*, a novel, *Apricots From Chernobyl*, a collection of essays, and *Bricks*, a collection of stories, will be published in 1995 and 1996 by Graywolf Press. He teaches creative writing at the University of Cincinnati.

BEN NYBERG teaches creative writing at Kansas State University, and he is the editor of *Kansas Quarterly*. His essay titled "Why Stories Fail" is part of the instructional book he is currently writing.

EDNA O'BRIEN has published novels, collections of stories and a play. Her most recent novel is *Time and Tide*, published by Warner Books. This year Warner Books published *An Edna O'Brien Reader*.

ADRIENNE RICH has published more than fifteen volumes of poems since her first collection, *Change of World*, won the Yale Series of Younger Poets Award in 1951. She has also published two collections of essays and speeches. Her feminist study of motherhood, *Of Woman Born: Motherhood as Experience and Institution*, was published by W.W. Norton.

NATALIA RACHEL SINGER's nonfiction and fiction have been published in *Harper's*, *Helicon Nine*, the *North American Review*, the *Seattle Post-Intelligence* and *Sundog*. In 1992 she won the World's Best Short Story Contest and was a finalist in 1993. She is an assistant professor of English at St. Lawrence University. Her essay "Nonfiction in the First Person, Without Apology" is a version of a talk she gave at St. Lawrence when she was applying for the job.

KIM R. STAFFORD is the author of *Having Everything Right: Essays of Place* and *Lochsa Road: A Pilgrim in the West*, both published by Confluence Press, and *Places and Stories*, published as part of the Carnegie-Mellon Poetry Series. He teaches creative writing at Lewis and Clark College in Portland, Oregon.

SHARON OARD WARNER's stories have appeared in a number of literary magazines. Her short story collection, *Learning to Dance*, won the Minnesota Voices Project and was published in 1992 by New Rivers Press. Presently, she's completing a novel.

MILLER WILLIAMS has written twenty-six books, including (with James Alan McPherson) a history of American railroads. His volumes of poetry include *Living on the Surface: New and Selected Poems*, published by Louisiana State University Press, and *Adjusting to the Light*, published by University of Missouri Press.

INDEX

ABOUT THE EDITOR

JACK HEFFRON is senior editor of Story Press and former associate editor of *Story* magazine. His short stories have appeared in such literary journals as *High Plains Literary Review, North American Review* and *TriQuarterly*. His book reviews have appeared in *Black Warrior Review* and *Utne Reader*. He lives in Cincinnati, Ohio.